Ethical Issues in Forensic
Mental Health Research

Forensic Focus

This series, edited by Gwen Adshead, *takes the field of Forensic Psychotherapy as its focal point, offering a forum for the presentation of theoretical and clinical issues. It embraces such influential neighbouring disciplines as language, law, literature, criminology, ethics and philosophy, as well as psychiatry and psychology, its established progenitors. Gwen Adshead is Consultant Forensic Psychotherapist and Lecturer in Forensic Psychotherapy at Broadmoor Hospital.*

Forensic Focus 21

Ethical Issues in Forensic Mental Health Research

Edited by Gwen Adshead and Christine Brown

Jessica Kingsley Publishers
London and New York

First published in the United Kingdom in 2003
by Jessica Kingsley Publishers Ltd
116 Pentonville Road
London N1 9JB, England
and
29 West 35th Street, 10th fl.
New York, NY 10001-2299

www.jkp.com

Copyright © Jessica Kingsley Publishers 2003

Library of Congress Cataloging in Publication Data
A CIP catalog record for this book is available from the Library of Congress

British Library Cataloguing in Publication Data
A CIP catalogue record for this book is available from the British Library

ISBN 1 84310 031 2

Printed and Bound in Great Britain
by Athenaeum Press, Gateshead, Tyne and Wear

Contents

Introduction

Gwen Adshead and Christine Brown

This book is based on a series of seminars run by the National Programme for Forensic Mental Health. Over two years, a group of researchers awarded Robert Baxter Fellowships (Baxter Fellows) met monthly to discuss the ethical dilemmas raised by the entire research process in which they were involved. We explored, in group discussion, questions of moral value and ethical practice in relation to the *conceptual* basis of the research idea, the *process* of carrying out the study, and its *outcome*. Different researchers using different methodologies often found that similar ethical problems came up; we also found that different conceptualisations of research methodology posed ethical dilemmas that challenged the conventional biomedical framework.

In this book, we have collated and re-presented the workings of the seminar group, which was generally given positive feedback by its members. We felt that it would be valuable to record and present an account of our discussions; not least because there seemed to be no other sources of information that concentrated on the ethical issues raised by research work in forensic mental health settings. Most existing work about research ethics does not offer much guidance about how to think about, say, the meaning of 'consent' in people who are both deprived of liberty and have reduced autonomy as a result of mental disorders. Nor is there much discussion in the bioethics literature about the value of research that offers benefit not to the participant concerned, or even people like him, but to possible future people who might be victims of participants.

There have been some important policy and administrative developments in relation to ethics and research that were not in place at the time of the seminars. Last year the Department of Health has published a detailed account of its research governance framework (Department of Health 2001c), following the publication of the Griffiths Report (NHS Executive 2000), and the Redfern Report (2001) into events at Alder Hey hospital. Guidelines have been published in relation to obtaining consent to treatment that include some advice about research consent (Department of Health 2001b) and about the application of research governance to ethics committees (Department of Health 2001a). All these documents explicitly state that ethical reasoning and understanding contribute directly to the quality of research, in concept and in practice.

It has also been an interesting time for forensic mental health research. There are more opportunities for funding than before, which suggests increased recognition of the mental health needs of users of forensic services. There is now a formal study group of academics in forensic psychiatry, which meets regularly to compare ideas; and new funding opportunities have particularly emphasised the development of new talent. The Government has indicated a willingness to support relevant research; although it must be said that this is likely to be linked with the proposals for services for dangerous and severe personality disorder, which might well be considered a researcher's poisoned chalice. Other difficulties include uncertainties about the application of research governance to forensic settings (for example, how do we involve forensic patients in the design and conduct of our research?) and the need to develop cross-disciplinary research projects, which are often hard to fund, and do not fit well with the current evaluative frameworks for biomedical research.

Carrying out research into forensic mental health raises complex and stimulating questions of value. The aim of the ethics seminars was to try and improve the quality of the answers – answers that will have to be given. The questions are not philosophical hypotheses; they are real-world dilemmas that have to be engaged with by researchers. We hope that newcomers to the field of forensic research will find this book helpful in planning their research; and that experienced researchers will use this book as a way of reflecting on their current and past practice.

There are several people who provided us with help and assistance in putting this book together, and we would like to acknowledge their contribution. We are very grateful to the National Programme for Forensic Mental Health for asking Gwen to run the seminars, and for providing the funding which made writing the book possible. In particular, we are grateful for the support of Dilys Jones, Professor Marshall Marinker, Kate Walker, Victoria Hyams and Kathryn Harney: all of whom took this project seriously and gave advice and help at different stages. We also thank the men of the Ferris household, who gave up maternal and uxorial support while this book was being put together – especially Jack (aged 20 months), who lacked capacity to give valid informed consent, and therefore had to give his consent by proxy.

NOTE

For ease of reading, the majority of patients and practitioners are referred to in the masculine.

REFERENCES

Department of Health (2001a) *Governance Arrangements for NHS Research Ethics Committees.* London: Central Office for Research Ethics Committees.

Department of Health (2001b) *Reference Guide to Consent for Examination and Treatment. London: Department of Health.*

Department of Health (2001c) *Research Governance Framework for Health and Social Care. London: Department of Health.*

NHS Executive (2000) *Report of a Review of the Research Framework in North Staffordshire Hospital NHS Trust (Griffiths Report).* West Midlands: NHSE.

Redfern Inquiry (2001) *Report of the Inquiry into Events at Alder Hey, Royal Liverpool Children's Hospital.* www.ricinquiry.org.uk/index.htm.

CHAPTER 1

Do You Feel Lucky?

Assessing Capacity to Consent to Research in Forensic Mental Health Practice

Gwen Adshead

I want to argue that decisions about having treatment for a condition and decisions about participating in research about a condition are different kinds of decision, and represent two different types of choice.

INVOLVING FORENSIC PATIENTS IN RESEARCH: CONSTRAINTS ON CONSENT

How are we to think about the decision making processes that take place when a forensic patient is asked to consent to participate in research? In both legal and moral terms, valid consent must be given freely, by a competent agent, who is informed about the procedure to which he is consenting (Kennedy and Grubb 1994). Legal argument, both here and in the USA, has arisen in relation to the operational criteria for competence, what aspects of detention might compromise freedom to choose, and the degree of information needed by participants to make a valid choice.

Feinberg considers the question of coercion and consent using the example of involving prisoners who volunteer to participate in research (Feinberg 1986). He concludes that prisoners who were offered a financial reward for participating in research were giving a form of 'counterfeit consent'. This is on three grounds: first, that the disparities of power increase the temptation to coercion and the likelihood of abuse; second, that it is repugnant to treat humans as mere subjects even with consent; and, third, that research may be a type of non-coercive exploitation which results in an unjust gain for researchers.

On Feinberg's argument, the presence of any constraints on freedom to choose would make it difficult to justify the involvement of detained individuals in research. Potential participants in forensic mental health research face similar constraints to prisoners in relation to participation in research. They are subject to real disparities of power in terms of legally sanctioned loss of liberty and indefinite detention i.e. a type of *external* constraint on choice making. Also, they may suffer a type of *internal* constraint as a result of the mental disorders or disabilities from which they suffer, and which are thought to give rise to the rule-breaking behaviour which in turn justifies the social sanctions and loss of liberty on the grounds of societal protection (Adshead 1997). The external constraints on their freedom are also justified on the therapeutic grounds of individual welfare rather than social defence – the use of which Kittrie called the 'therapeutic state' (1971).

Feinberg would argue that the forensic patient's capacity to consent – that is, the capacity to freely choose – is vitiated by both the internal and the external constraints which exist. How, then, to argue that forensic patients can consent in a way which is meaningful?

CONSENT OF FORENSIC PATIENTS TO RESEARCH PARTICIPATION

Positive arguments for involving forensic patients in research take a number of different forms. The first set of arguments draws on the status of forensic patients as 'volunteers' generally. Although the choice-making processes of patients may be constrained to some degree by their mental conditions, nevertheless they are generally competent to make a sufficiently free choice. The law in relation to consent to *treatment* reflects this general assumption, and spells out some of the parameters. In the USA, this has taken a formal structure called 'informed consent', usually involving a written statement read and signed by the patient. Equally in English law, the giving of consent to treatment protects the doctor from any subsequent claims that the touching was unlawful.

The expression of consent is not sufficient in law if the patient is not competent to take that decision. Recent English case law has set out the criteria for mental fitness to make a treatment decision (*Re C* 1994):

- Can the patient take in the information?
- Can he believe it?
- Can he weigh up the information and make a decision?

If the answer to these questions is yes, then the patient is free to make a decision about treatment (either acceptance or refusal); this decision must be accepted regardless of the consequences for the patient (*St Georges* v. *S.* 1998).

What some authors have argued is that if patients are fit to consent to treatment, then they can consent to research participation. This implies that the decision to have treatment is similar to whether or not to participate in research. If people are assumed to be able to choose to accept or refuse treatment given the right degree of information and an absence of coercion from others, then forensic patients also should not be assumed to lack competence just because they are either mentally ill or detained.

Other arguments which support the involvement of forensic patients in research emphasise the benefits. First, unless patients do participate, there will be no research, and the benefits of research, both now and in the future, provide a strong motive for patient participation. Second, it is sometimes argued that patients should participate in research, and have a duty to do so, as citizens. A variation on this argument is the view that contribution to social activities such as research is a benefit to individuals, and that this benefit should not be kept from anyone, even people who have lost their liberty as a result of offending. Researchers therefore have a duty to help patients participate in research; either because it is every citizen's duty to participate, or because it may be of benefit to the participant (Gunn and Taylor 1993).

INCOMPETENT PATIENTS AND RESEARCH

Most debate about research in psychiatry has centred around the involvement of incompetent patients in research. The Nuremberg Code of Ethics in Medical Research, devised in 1947, stated that all participants must give free consent to participation in research, if the research process was to be ethically justifiable. Subsequent codes of ethics have taken the same position, which could result in psychiatric patients (whose conditions most commonly affect competence) being excluded from research. In such a case, this might lead to an absence of research into the conditions causing the incompetence, which might not be a problem for the patients themselves, but might reduce the chances of preventing or ameliorating the condition for future patients.

The loss of the chance to obtain future benefits, or prevent future harms, has led to the argument that the involvement of incompetent patients in research could be ethically justifiable on certain conditions. Various codes of ethics and advisory papers have taken the view that the moral wrongness of getting someone to comply with a research procedure without his consent is justified if, and only if, the possible harm is very small and the possible benefit to others is very great (World Medical Assembly 2000). Therefore, great attention must be paid to the assessment of risks and benefits of the proposed research and the question of who is being asked to take risks and who will be receiving the benefits.

THERAPEUTIC AND NON-THERAPEUTIC RESEARCH

There are research procedures which may be of direct benefit to the participant, such as drug trials or innovative treatments. Note that there does not *have* to be benefit to the patient, only a possibility of benefit. Such research is commonly referred to as 'therapeutic' research, and the involvement of incompetent patients in this type of research seems less ethically questionable, given the criteria above. Such research may involve acutely ill patients whose condition is under investigation, and whose participation is essential for the research to occur.

However, there has been much more concern about the involvement of incompetent patients in research procedures which cannot and will never be of any benefit to them, but may benefit others. Helmchen has termed this the 'instrumentalisation' of patients (1998). Such 'non-therapeutic research' makes use of the patient's condition to gain knowledge for the researchers and possible benefit for future patients. The incompetent patient becomes a means to an end in which he has no immediate stake or interest. In response to this problem, most codes and advice have concluded that it may still be morally justifiable to involve incompetent patients in non-therapeutic research, if the criteria above are satisfied, if there is no other group of patients who can be involved, and there has been some form of external review of the project by an independent group of experts. Legally, this position in English law is not so open; most legal argument has concluded that it is not lawful to involve incompetent patients in any research process unless that process also has a therapeutic aim (Kennedy and Grubb 1994, p.1065).

Within general psychiatry, the patient groups who are most likely to be made incompetent to participate in research by their conditions are those people with dementia or learning disabilities i.e. where there is some degree of enduring neurological impairment. The assessment of competence is complex, and cannot be discussed here in any depth: interested readers are referred to Grisso and Appelbaum (1998), or the British Medical Association's guidance (1995). However, it is by no means clear that mental illness or learning disability makes people incompetent to take consent decisions, including consent to research participation (Appelbaum *et al.* 1999; Carpenter *et al.* 2000; Gunn *et al.* 1999; Pinals *et al.* 1997). In fact, it could be argued that other factors, relating more to social myths about doctor–patient relationships, impair competence more than symptoms of mental illness (Appelbaum *et al.* 1987).

Most forensic patients do not suffer from the kind of conditions which would permanently impair their capacity to consent to research participation. They suffer from a wide range of disorders, which may or may not affect their capacity to consent to research. The use of standardised assessment tools, such as the MacCAT-R (Carpenter *et al.* 2000) may provide more empirical data on this point. For example, we have little or no data about the competence of people with personality disorders (a substantial minority within forensic populations) to consent to research participation. It is likely that there is a variety of social and environmental factors (as opposed to psychological and biological) that may affect the competence of forensic patients to consent to research participation. These would include the setting in which they are detained, the nature of their detention, their attitude to detention and their relationship with the researcher.

CONSENT TO TREATMENT AND CONSENT TO RESEARCH: ARE THEY THE SAME?

I want now to turn to compare the decision making processes involved in consent to treatment and research. The suggestion that therapy and research are the same procedure for the patient, and competence to consent to one implies competence to consent to the other, seems implausible on a number of counts. Most legal jurisdictions specify the need for separate consents to research precisely because the procedures are seen to be different. The therapeutic/non-therapeutic research distinction, which has existed since 1931 (Sass 1988), assumes that there is a difference between therapy and research. Where, then, does the difference lie?

Intentions of the researcher

Primarily, the difference must lie in the intention of the researcher. A therapeutic procedure is intended to benefit an identified patient in the mind of the clinician, in the immediate or short term.

It has been argued that even in the case of therapeutic research, the primary intention of that research is not the immediate benefit of the patient-participant (Fulford and Howse 1993; Gillon 2001, p.258). In some cases, the trial therapeutic procedure may bring no immediate or long-term benefit to the patient-participant at all. If there is a direct benefit to the patient-participant, this benefit is not necessarily the intended outcome of the research, but rather is a side-effect of the process. One might consider this to be an empirical version of the principle of double effect: the researcher does not intend to benefit the patient, but the procedure has a good chance of so doing.

Decision making processes for the patient and the participant are therefore different. In ordinary clinical decision making, the patient will wish to consider the information about benefits for him, as provided by his doctor. In the ordinary treatment setting, the patient can feel a type of confidence that he is the primary object of his doctor's beneficence. He need not be the *sole* object – the doctor's duties to third parties will also be a relevant consideration – but he can claim a type of primacy, which is personal to him. Equally, the patient may be constrained in making a choice by his dependence and neediness of the clinician. The patient needs the treatment, and may be so constrained by that need that his willingness or ability to refuse is vitiated. This is not the same as lacking capacity: it is an acknowledgement that fear, dependency and need alter the relationship between doctor and patient

Participation in research arguably involves the patient in a different decision. The words themselves give some hint of the difference; the 'patient' undergoes or suffers something, which may be painful or distressing, and is at least intrusive. The consent of the patient shares the responsibility for the patient with the doctor. By contrast, the 'participant' may be seen as taking more responsibility for his own decision: the degree of shared responsibility is different. The researcher is not absolved of responsibility, but there is perhaps more of a sense of shared responsibility with a volunteer.

Relationship between participant and researcher

Another way to think about the differences between therapy and research lies in the nature of the relationships between the protagonists. The doctor–patient relationship is a complex transaction, affected by many factors including the duration of the relationship, the depth and quality of the engagement in terms of trust and empathy, and the degree of mutuality or appreciation of each other's position (Cox 1978). Time, depth and mutuality are likely to be very different for the relationship between the researcher and the would-be participant; the participant may not know the researcher at all, and the depth of the engagement focuses on the intentions of the research and the researcher, not the patient. In such circumstances, the quality of mutuality will be different: not better or worse necessarily, but different.

I am not suggesting that researchers do not care for their participants, only that their relationship with the participants would be different if they were their therapists. This distinction has been made elsewhere, making the point that clinicians and researchers should be different people, so that there is no confusion of role (World Medical Assembly 2000). Thornton (1994) points out that she felt differently about the clinician who changed from 'her' doctor to a researcher.

It is also useful to consider the use of the language involved in these different relationships, and the significance in terms of agency: is a research subject like the subject of a king? Is a patient one to whom things are done? Is a participant the same as a volunteer (Walsh-Bowers 1995)?

CONSENTING TO RESEARCH: CHOOSING TO GAMBLE

One way to think about what happens when people choose to participate in research is that they choose to take a chance, to gamble. This argument can be seen indirectly in the language used in some papers on human research and consent. Engelhardt (1988) talks of participants 'playing the odds'. When the researcher invites the patient to participate, the patient is being invited to take a chance – a chance that taking part in this procedure may not do him any good and may even cause some discomfort or harm. He is also invited to take a chance that involvement will benefit others – to gamble that the researcher's intention and hopes will be fulfilled. Of course, the chances may be very good that the participant will benefit, and very slight that harm will befall, and the participant has to trust the researcher that this is so. Nevertheless, the choice-making procedure is not simply one of agreeing to participate, but consenting to take a chance, and consenting to balance up the risk to self against the benefit to self and others.

CONSENTING TO RESEARCH: CHOOSING TO BE NICE

Furthermore, in non-therapeutic research, the participant is being asked to gamble on a procedure which not only asks something from him but also provides no benefit, and this is requested on the grounds of benefit to possible others. This is arguably a request to gamble on altruistic grounds; will you consider taking a chance in order to benefit another person? Clearly, the participant will want to consider the risks to himself, but this is a decisional step. The thinking process involved in the choice/intention to benefit another is surely different from the thinking processes involved in appreciating risks and benefits to the self.

COMPETENCY TO CONSENT FOR RESEARCH

On these grounds, therefore, it seems that deciding to undergo a course of treatment is a very different decision making process from deciding to participate in research. The choices involved in research participation involve both the decision to gamble and the decision to be altruistic. Recent research into assessment of competence in the area of mental health similarly distinguishes treatment consent and research consent, so that the MacArthur project on competence assessment separates competence to consent to treatment (MacCAT-T) and competence to consent to research

(MacCAT-R). The MacCAT-R however does not address the question of the capacity either to gamble or to make an altruistic decision.

ALTRUISTIC CAPACITY

Competence to be altruistic might be seen as a complex mental capacity, involving as it does imagination, empathy, a sense of time and an appreciation of beneficence (see Berghmanns 1998). On these grounds it might be argued that many mentally ill patients will not possess such a high degree of competence. The counterargument suggests that such pro-social attitudes appear early developmentally and are present in most children by ages three to four.

However, one real difficulty in forensic settings is that the capacity to make altruistic decisions may be the capacity which is most impaired and is the cause of their detention for many patients (Hare 1999). There may then be real difficulties not only in recruitment of participants, but the extent to which refusal may bias the sample. In my own research with Jonathan Glover on moral reasoning, it has been impossible to know whether those most lacking in the capacity to make moral decisions were most likely to refuse to participate. Equally, researching this capacity may be problematic.

Assessment of decision making capacity has always involved a consideration not only of the consequences of the decision, but also the reasoning processes behind the decision (Roth, Meisel and Lidz 1977). Charland (1998) argues that the basis of competence is 'recognisable reasons'; why people make the decisions they do is important. Fethe (1993) offers an analysis of the capacity to volunteer, and is critical of Jonas' view that assessments of the motives for volunteering are reasonably simple. He suggests that there might be as many negative reasons for volunteering as positive; a point which is made in a study of parents who volunteered their children for research (Harth et al. 1992). Parents in this study were more likely to be depressed, lacking in confidence and compliant than parents who did not volunteer their children.

Thus mental conditions which might affect competence to take research participation decisions include not only the obvious conditions like chronic psychotic states, or major affective disorder, but also personality disorders which affect perceptions of coercion and compliance. Past experiences of interpersonal violence (either in childhood or in adulthood) may make the patient hypersensitive to threat perception, or the consequences of failing to please authority figures. It might even be argued that patients with personality disorders have such a fragmented sense of self, and diminished sense of self-worth, that the capacity to assess and weigh up risk to self against benefit to others is limited. This is especially so if we understand competence to take any form of decision as including knowing, understanding and doing (Roth, Meisel and Lidz 1977).

COERCION REVISITED

Finally, there is the effect of detention on choice making to consider. If making ordinary decisions is hard when one is externally constrained, how much more difficult is it when the decisions are complex ones, like the decision to gamble? Nor is it clear what it might mean to a person whose liberty has been taken away by society, as a punishment, to be asked to be socially altruistic, even if there is some benefit to them (Hornblum 1999).

Much of the uneasiness that is felt about prisoner or detained patient involvement in research may relate to a concern about exploitation of the vulnerable; an activity which many prisoners and forensic patients have taken part in, and the reason why they are detained. If researchers exploit such people simply because it is possible to do so, then this is a mirror of the exploitation that caused harm in the first place. How can we exhort forensic patients and prisoners not to use other people merely as means if we as researchers plan to do it ourselves?

COUNTERARGUMENTS: CONSENT IS CONSENT

I would argue that the case for distinguishing therapy and research procedures is strong – yet this is not a distinction which is commonly made in the literature on consent and the mentally ill. Many chapters, books and articles seem to suggest that if an individual can consent to treatment, then he is fit to consent to research.

Some might argue that all medical decisions are a type of gamble, including treatment decision; there are no guarantees. To this point, one might respond by bringing in the intention of the professional; a gamble taken at the advice of someone who has your interests as a primary concern is rather different to a gamble taken on the advice of someone who doesn't.

IS THERE A DUTY TO PARTICIPATE IN RESEARCH?

It has often been suggested that there is a duty on citizens to participate in research – in effect, to show some degree of altruism (Baum 1994; Lindley 2001). This argument seems particularly to have been applied to NHS patients, where there is an elision of citizenship with NHS patienthood: if one receives social benefits, this implies reciprocal responsibility to contribute to those benefits (Ashcroft 2001). Research with possible participants indicates that many people do perceive a duty to take part in research (Russell, Moralejo and Burgess 2000); an editorial in the *American Journal of Psychiatry* suggested that there might be a right to run risks for rewards (Appelbaum 1998). Presumably this right arises from some account of social inclusion and reciprocal benefits. If this right is the right to make the choice to run risks, then this looks like a suggested right to gamble.

The counterarguments are both general and specific. At a general level, if volunteering/participation is understood as altruistic, and that altruism is rewarded as a virtue which not everybody shows, then it seems hard to argue that there is a duty to be virtuous, *simpliciter*. Of course, there are many moral codes (including most of the world's religious belief systems) that would argue that there is a duty to be virtuous, but at the same time, the possibility of choosing not to be virtuous has to remain to give the choice to be virtuous its positive connotation (Ashcroft 2001). Equally, as Gillon suggests (2001), a duty to volunteer is not the same as a duty on others to make you volunteer; nor is there any obvious reason why incompetent individuals may be compelled to be virtuous by others, whereas competent individuals cannot be.

Specifically, there might be real concerns about applying a duty to participate to forensic patients. Again, duties to engage in socially beneficial activities, based on the notion of reciprocal interests, might not apply to those who have already been excluded from social responsibilities and duties on the grounds of social condemnation. This might apply less to offenders who were not detained, where a duty to participate in research might be understood as a reciprocal benefit in not being detained, and therefore being free to make good the social harm that was done. Where society has punished someone by removing his liberty to be a social animal, it seems hard to argue that he retains all his normal social duties. Equally, where liberty has been removed on the grounds of therapeutic benefit to the individual (and reduction of risk to others), the patient is no longer free to exercise social duties; in fact, his illness itself would normally be seen as grounds for relieving him of his social duties (Parsons 1951).

If it were the case that forensic patients lack the capacity to fulfil their social duties and act altruistically and that this was the locus of their incompetence, it would therefore seem odd to compel someone to do something of which he is not capable. There might also be real social concerns about doctors making people 'be nice'. This concern already exists in forensic psychiatry, where it is sometimes not clear whether the therapeutic aim is to make people feel better or behave better (Adshead 2000, *JME*).

WHO GUARDS THE GUARDIANS? RESEARCH CODES AND ETHICS

It is perhaps noteworthy that most papers addressing the issue of the involvement of non-competent psychiatric patients in research are written by psychiatric researchers, who seem inevitably to conclude that non-competent patients must be allowed and should be allowed to participate in research. The researchers' main argument is a consequentialist one: if non-competent patients are excluded from research, then this will be bad for science (and certainly for the careers of the researchers). Hence, researchers may be keen to play down ethical concerns about forensic research, as evidenced by this statement from a forensic psychiatric textbook (Gunn and Taylor 1993): 'All research is ethical unless it can be shown to be otherwise.' This statement presumes that it is the job of the Local Research Ethics Committee (LREC) to demonstrate that a protocol is not ethically justified. However, LRECs consider that the burden of proof lies with the researchers applying for ethical approval.

There is an argument for involving incompetent psychiatric patients in research, which rests not in terms of benefits to others, or in terms of social duties, but in terms of proxy consent. One could argue that one aspect of autonomy is a relational autonomy, especially in cases of chronic and long-term disability (Agich 1993). Autonomy on this account is not about complete independence, but about choices being located in a network of relationships that support the dependent person. On these grounds, it might be argued that ethically, if not legally, a carer who knows the patient well could give his consent to participate by proxy (given the usual caveats about minimal risk or discomfort).

This argument will not deal with all of the concerns detailed above about lack of consent, and involvement in research. Incompetent detained forensic patients are a vulnerable group on both mental illness and detention grounds, and arguably have greater claims to protection than ordinary psychiatric patients. There is scope however for more research into what it is to be competent to consent, and the process of getting consent itself (as described by Gunn *et al.* 1999, 2000) and the experience of research by participants. There are studies which indicate that participation in research can be a positive experience (Brody 1998; Marshall *et al.* 2001); such studies have not been carried out in forensic populations.

Recently, it has been argued that there is little validity in the distinction between therapeutic research and non-therapeutic research, in terms of risks and benefits (Dickenson and Fulford, 2000; Royal College of Psychiatrists, 2000; World Medical Assembly 2000) and that this distinction should be 'removed'. Murphy (1988) also suggests that research is part of a clinician's therapeutic role, and that the distinction may mean little. The counterargument rests on the question of intention; there may indeed be little distinction in terms of consequences, but arguably a significant distinction in terms of researcher intention (Gillon 1992). Fennell (2001) describes the distinction as 'crucial' and several other documents have continued to maintain it (e.g. the Mental Health Act Commission1997). Kennedy and Grubb (1994) cite the philosopher Hare (p.1031) who defines the distinction between therapeutic and non-therapeutic research solely in terms of intention, and not consequences. Even if one did focus only on risky consequences (which in my view is *not* why therapeutic research is favoured over non-therapeutic), we know that risks may be hard to communicate with patients (Calman 1996). Even if the distinction were removed (and it is hard to see how an argument can be 'removed'), there would still be the question of whether and to what extent any potential research participant was able to take a gamble: to ask himself the question, 'Do I feel lucky?'

CONCLUSION

Arguably much of the literature on consent to research is biased, written as it is by a highly selected sample of researchers, who may stand to gain most immediate benefit from the research process (Bartlett 1992; Sheikh 2000). Perhaps what would be most helpful would be more training in moral reasoning for researchers, especially as awareness and concern about research misconduct is growing. Ethical guidelines may have no effect on the conduct of research; as Nicholson (1988) points out, guidelines that prohibited research without the consent of the participant existed in Germany in 1931. Specifically in relation to forensic research, codes may be of little help in addressing dilemmas of confidentiality (Monahan *et al.* 1993). Increased awareness of ethical complexity in mental health research generally may be the best place to start; it is salutary to note that neither an early paper on research in delinquency nor a very recent paper on randomised controlled trials (RCTs) in psychiatry mention anything about ethical problems (Andrews 1999; Gibbens 1966).

SUMMARY

- Consent to research involves an interaction between patient and researcher that is different from a therapeutic encounter both by the intention of the researcher and the relationship between the researcher and the patient. The degree of responsibility of the researcher for the patient's wellbeing is vitiated by the patient's voluntary participation having made a balanced decision about the risks and benefits of taking part.

- Consent to participate in research is different from consent to treatment.

- Therefore, capacity to consent to research is different from capacity to consent to treatment.

- To give consent to research, a patient is choosing to take a risk that he will not be harmed but may benefit from the research or that others may benefit from the research.

- There needs to be a specific consideration of forensic patients' capacity to consent to research, given their particular external and internal constraints on choice.

CODES, GUIDELINES AND ADVISORY DOCUMENTS REVIEWED

CIOMS (1993) *International Ethical Guidelines for Biomedical Research Involving Human Subjects.* Geneva: CIOMS/WHO.

Law Commission (1993) *Mentally Incapacitated Adults and Decision Making: Medical Treatment and Research. Consultation Paper 129.* London: HMSO.

Medical Research Council (1991) *Working Party on Research on the Mentally Incapacitated.* London: MRC www.mrc.ac.uk/ethics.

Mental Health Act Commission (1997) *Research Involving Detained Patients. Position Paper 1.* Nottingham: MHAC.

Nuremberg Code (1947) Reprinted in M.Parker and D. Dickenson (eds) (2001) *The Cambridge Medical Ethics Workbook.* Cambridge: CUP, 115.

Royal College of Physicians (1996) *Guidelines on the Practice of Ethics Committees in Medical Research Involving Humans.* (3rd edition.) London: RCP.

Royal College of Psychiatrists (2000) *Guidelines for Researchers and Research Ethics Committees on Psychiatric Research Involving Human Participants.* London: Royal College of Psychiatrists.

World Medical Assembly (1964) 'Recommendations Guiding Doctors in Biomedical Research Involving Human Subjects. (Helsinki Declaration).' In J. Gunn and P. Taylor (eds) (1993) *Forensic Psychiatry: Clinical, Legal and Ethical Issues.* London: Butterworth Heinemann.

World Medical Assembly (2000) *Fifth Revision of the Helsinki Declaration.* Madrid: WMA. www.wma.net.

REFERENCES

Adshead, G. (1997) 'Informed Consent and Psychiatric Research.' *Annales Instituto Superiore Sanita 33*, 4, 497–503.

Adshead, G. (2000) 'Care or Custody? Ethical Dilemmas in Forensic Psychiatry.' *Journal of Medical Ethics 26*, 302–304.

Agich, G. (1993) *Autonomy and Long Term Care.* Oxford: OUP.

Andrews, G. (1999) 'RCTs in Psychiatry: Important but Poorly Accepted.' *BMJ, 319*, 562–564.

Appelbaum, P. (1998) 'Missing the Boat: Competence and Consent in Psychiatric Research.' *American Journal of Psychiatry, 155*, 1468–1489.

Appelbaum, P., Grisso, T., Ellen, F., O'Donnell, S. and Kupfer, D. J. (1999) 'Competence of Depressed Patients to Consent to Research.' *American Journal of Psychiatry, 156*, 1380–1384.

Appelbaum, P. S., Roth, L., Lidz, C., Benson, P. and Winslade, W. (1987) 'False Hopes and Best Data: Consent to Research and the Therapeutic Misconception.' *Hastings Center Report* April, 20–24.

Ashcroft, R. (2001) 'Autonomy and Informed Consent in the Ethics of the RCT: Philosophical Perspectives.' In M. Parker and D. Dickenson (eds) *The Cambridge Medical Ethics Workbook.* Cambridge: CUP, 94.

Bartlett, A. (1992) 'Ethics and Psychiatric Research.' *Psychiatric Bulletin, 19,* 670–672.

Baum, M. (1994) 'Response to Thornton.' *JME,* 20, 23–25.

Berghmanns, R. (1998) 'Advance Directives for Non-therapeutic Dementia Research: Some Ethical and Policy Considerations.' *JME,* 24, 32–37.

British Medical Association (1995) *Assessment of Mental Capacity.* London: BMA Books.

Brody, B. (1998) *The Ethics of Biomedical Research.* New York and Oxford: OUP.

Calman, K. (1996) 'Cancer: Science, Society and the Communication of Risk.' *BMJ,* 313, 799–802.

Carpenter, W., Gold, L., Lahti, A., Queern, C., Conley, R., Bartko, J., Kovnick, J. and Appelbaum, P. (2000) 'Decisional Capacity for Informed Consent in SCP Research.' *Arch Gen Psych,* 57, 533–538.

Charland, L. (1998) 'Is Mr Spock Mentally Competent? Competence to Consent and Emotion.' *Philosophy, Psychiatry and Psychology,* 5, 67–82.

Cox, M. (1978) *Structuring the Therapeutic Process: Compromise with Chaos.* London: JKP.

Dickenson, D. and Fulford, K.W. (2000) *In Two Minds: A Casebook of Psychiatric Ethics.* Oxford: OUP.

Doyal, L. and Tobias, J. (eds) (2001) *Informed Consent in Medical Research.* London: BMJ Books.

Engelhardt, T. (1988) 'Diagnosing Well and Treating Prudently: The RCT and the Problem of Knowing Truly.' In S. F. Spicker *et al.* (eds) *The Use of Human Beings in Research.* London: Kluwer.

Feinberg, J. (1986) *Harm to Self: The Moral Limits of the Criminal Law.* Oxford: OUP.

Fennell, P. (2001) 'Informed Consent and Clinical Research in Psychiatry.' In L. Doyal and J. Tobias (eds) *Informed Consent in Medical Research.* London: BMJ Books, 183–191.

Fethe, C. (1993) 'Beyond Voluntary Consent: Hans Jonas on the Moral Requirements of Human Experimentation.' *JME,* 19, 99–103.

Fulford, K. W. M. and Howse, K. (1993) 'Ethics of Research with Psychiatric Patients: Principles, Problems and the Primary Responsibilities of Research.' *JME*, 19, 85–91.

Gibbens, T. (1966) 'Psychiatric Research in Delinquency Behaviour.' *BMJ*, 2, 695–698.

Gillon, R. (1992) 'Editorial.' *Journal of Medical Ethics*, 18, 59–60.

Gillon, R. (2001) '"Fully" Informed Consent, Clinical Trials and the Boundaries of Therapeutic Discretion.' In L. Doyal and J. Tobias *Informed Consent in Medical Research*. London: BMJ Books, 258–265.

Grisso, T and Appelbaum, P. (1998) *Assessing Competence to Consent to Treatment*. Oxford: OUP.

Gunn, J and Taylor, P. (eds) (1993) *Forensic Psychiatry: Clinical, Legal and Ethical Issues*. London: Butterworth Heinemann.

Gunn, M., Wong, J., Clare, I. and Holland, A. (1999) 'Decision Making Capacity.' *MedLaw Review*, 7, 269–306.

Gunn, M., Wong, J., Clare, I. and Holland, A. (2000) 'Medical Research and Incompetent Adults.' *Journal of Mental Health Law*, 60–72.

Hare, R. (1999) 'Psychopathy as a Risk Factor for Violence.' *Psychiatric Quarterly, 70*, 181–197.

Harth, S. C., Johnstone, R. and Thong, Y. (1992) 'The Psychological Profile of Parents who Volunteer their Children for Clinical Research: A Controlled Study.' *Journal of Medical Ethics*, 18, 86–93.

Helmchen, H. (1998) 'Research with Incompetent Demented Patients. A Current Problem in Light of German History.' *European Psychiatry*, 13 (Supp. 3), 93–100.

Hewlett, S. (1996) 'Consent to Clinical Research – Adequately Voluntary or Substantially Influenced?' *JME*, 22, 232–237.

Hirsch, S and Harris, J. (eds) (1988) *Consent and the Incompetent Patient*. London: Gaskell, Royal College of Psychiatrists.

Hornblum, A. M. (1999) *Acres of Skin: Human Experiments at Holmesburg Prison*. London: Routledge.

Jonas, H. (1969) 'Philosophical Reflections on Experimenting with Human Subjects.' In T. Beauchamp and L. Walters (eds) *Contemporary Issues in Bioethics* (3rd edition). California: Wadsworth Publishing Co.

Kennedy, I. and Grubb, A. (1994) *Medical Law: Text with Materials*. London: Butterworth Heinemann.

Kittrie, N. (1971) *The Right to be Different: Deviance and Enforced Therapy*. London and New York: Johns Hopkins University Press.

Lindley, R. (2001) 'Thrombolytic Treatment for Acute Ischaemic Stroke: Consent can be Ethical.' In L. Doyal and J. Tobias (eds) *Informed Consent in Medical Research*. London: BMJ Books, 133–6.

McCubbin, M. and Cohen, D. (1996) 'Extremely Unbalanced: Interest Divergence and Power Disparities Between Clients and Psychiatrists.' *International Journal of Law and Psychiatry* 4, 19, 1–25.

Marshall, R. D., Spitzer, R. L., Vaughn, S., Vaughn, R., Mellman, L., MacKinnon, R. and Roose, S. (2001) 'Assessing the Subjective Experience of being a Participant in Research.' *American Journal of Psychiatry*, 158, 319–321.

Monahan, J., Appelbaum, P., Mulvey, E., Robbins, P. C. and Lidz, C. (1993) 'Ethical and Legal Duties in Conducting Research on Violence: Lessons from the MacArthur Risk Assessment Study.' *Violence and Victims*, 8, 387–396.

Murphy, E. (1988) 'Psychiatric Implications.' In S. Hirsch and J. Harris (eds) *Consent and the Incompetent Patient*. London: Gaskell, Royal College of Psychiatrists, 65–74.

Nicholson, R. (1988) 'Commentary.' In S. Hirsch and J. Harris (eds) *Consent and the Incompetent Patient*. London: Gaskell, Royal College of Psychiatrists, 96.

Ondrusek, N., Abramovitch, R., Pencharz, P. and Koren, G. (1998) 'Empirical Examination of the Ability of Children to Consent to Clinical Research.' *JME*, 24, 158–165.

Parker, M. and Dickenson, D. (2001) *The Cambridge Medical Ethics Workbook*. Cambridge: CUP.

Parsons, T. (1951) *The Social System*. London: Routledge.

Pinals, D., Malhotra, A. K., Breier, A. and Pickar, D. (1997) 'Informed Consent in SCp Research.' *Psychiatric Services*, 49, 244.

Roth, L., Meisel, A. and Lidz, C. (1977) 'Tests of Competence to Consent to Treatment.' *American Journal of Psychiatry*, 134, 279–243.

Russell, M., Moralejo, D. G. and Burgess, E. D. (2000) 'Paying Research Subjects: Participants' Perspectives.' *JME*, 26, 126–130.

Sass, H. (1988) 'Comparative Models and Goals for the Regulation of Human Research.' In S. F. Spicker *et al.* (eds) *The Use of Human Beings in Research*. London: Kluwer.

Sheikh, A. (2000) 'Publication Ethics.' *Journal of Medical Ethics*, 26, 422–427.

Silverman, W. A. (1989) 'The Myth of Informed Consent: In Daily Practice and Clinical Trials.' *JME*, 15, 6–11.

Spicker, S. F., Alon, I., de Vries, A. and Engelhardt, T. (1988) *The Use of Human Beings in Research.* London: Kluwer.

Sugarman, J., Kass, N., Goodman, S., Perentesis, P., Fernandes, P. and Faden, R. (1998) 'What Patients Say About Medical Research.' *IRB: A Review of Human Subjects Research,* 20, 1–7.

Thornton, H. (1994) 'Clinical Trials: A Brave New Partnership?' *JME,* 20, 19–22.

Walsh-Bowers, R. (1995) 'The Reporting and Ethics of the Research Relationship in Areas of Interpersonal Psychology.' *Theory and Psychology,* 5, 233–250.

CASES

Re C (Adult: Refusal of Medical Treatment) [1994] 1 All ER 819.
St George's Healthcare NHS Trusts v. *S.* [1998] 3 All ER 673.

CHAPTER 2

In Whose Best Interest?

Consent by Adolescents to Research Participation

Justine Rothwell and Carly Smith

BACKGROUND

The primary goal of all research is to obtain data (both quantitative and qualitative) in the most rigorous/disciplined manner possible and provide answers. However, there are a number of factors, both intrapersonal and interpersonal, that may influence the process of data collection in ways which reduce rigour and introduce bias. The influence of the researcher's own state of mind is crucial in determining what data will be selected or ignored, and how it will be interpreted. Other factors include the researcher being put off by practical difficulties in obtaining data, attempts to dismiss inconsistencies in the data by undertaking repeated evaluation, or the researcher's willingness to accept any co-occurrence as evidence of correlation.

All these intrapersonal factors introduce bias and reduce rigour. There are however other *interpersonal* factors that interfere with data collection and analysis, and these are often intimately connected with ethical issues and dilemmas about competing value systems. In this chapter we will look at the issue of consent and the obtaining of consent, based on one of the authors' experience of carrying out research in a forensic facility for young people.

We will examine the ethical issues surrounding the ability of young people to provide consent to participate in a research project: specifically issues of competence, the legal dilemmas facing the researcher/carer, good practice and the ability to refuse/withdraw consent. This chapter will also consider the complexities of establishing a research framework from a legal perspective in light of the *Gillick* case (1985), the Children and Young Person Act (Department of Health 1989) and the Mental Health Act (HMSO 1983). It will guide the reader through the conceptual aspects of establishing a research protocol, the obstacles and the potential impact of conflicts of interests between the young person and his carers.

There is growing recognition amongst practitioners and researchers of the importance of getting consent from patients to undertake both proven or novel treatment approaches or participate in research. The issues have in the last decade become highly sensitive, and to some extent can pose a political 'nightmare' for practitioners and researchers, who are often placed in the unenviable position of trying to advance knowledge alongside treating an individual in the best possible manner i.e. with respect and dignity. Much has been written regarding the numerous legal aspects of competence, consent, human rights and the protection of those who cannot protect themselves. The motives of clinicians who care for the vulnerable, and research practitioners who study their problems, are now more than ever the focus of public, professional and legal attention.

The process of consent

The *definition* of consent is wide but, for the purpose of guiding the reader, the definition quoted by Trudeau in 1993 will be the cornerstone of this chapter. Trudeau stated that consent was:

> A process by which an individual is provided with information pertaining to a specific treatment, and is then given the opportunity to accept or reject the treatment in part or in its entirety.

In this sense, consent is essential as an aspect of the basic need of all individuals (regardless of their level of cognitive ability) to be treated with dignity and respect. Getting consent is not only a legal requirement; it is an ethical imperative, especially for those groups of patients who are vulnerable because of their illness or their age.

For consent to be valid it must fulfil a number of criteria. The individual must be *capable* of consenting (which we discuss in more detail below). Consent must be given *freely* (which implies freedom from pressure), and must be given with the understanding of the benefits or costs to himself (which implies some degree of communication of *information*).

Definition of a child

Getting consent involves the patient in making a decision. In relation to children and young people, their capacity to make important medical and life decisions has received increasing media and academic attention as the understanding of the importance of the decision making process has increased. For practitioners and researchers wishing to engage children or young people in a treatment trial or research, it is essential to consider a number of factors about the defining category of the 'child', and how these relate to a young person's capacity to give consent to treatment or research.

Currently, in the United Kingdom, legal definition states that all young people under the age of 18 are to be considered a 'child'. The legal perspective illustrates that clear boundaries between childhood and adulthood do exist, but legal age differs from social and emotional age. These differences can lead to conflicts and confusion for young people about their roles, rights, responsibilities and expectations.

Most legal definitions of the capacity to give consent utilise age as the essential criterion. For example, the legal age of consent to sexual relationships is 16 for heterosexuals and 18 for homosexuals i.e. it is only at this age that the young person is deemed to have the requisite capacity to consent. In relation to the capacity to make medical treatment decisions, the legal age is 16. However, in the case of *Gillick* (1985), the House of Lords reviewed the criteria for the competence of children and young people to give consent to treatment. By the three to two majority, they argued that intellectual ability and age needed to be considered along with 'maturity', in order to determine a young person's level of competence. Thus children under 16 could make valid treatment choices if they were thought to be sufficiently mature – what is known now as 'Gillick competence'.

Where a young person is deemed not to have 'Gillick competence', a proxy consent has to be sought from a person with parental responsibility. Such a legal perspective illustrates that social criteria (such as age) do not mark clear boundaries between childhood/adolescence/adulthood and other ways of thinking about competence are needed. More recently it has been suggested that rather than defining the issue of consent by arbitary age cut-off points, there should be an awareness of the level of cognitive and emotional maturity and development (Booth 1994; Dickenson 1994). Cognitive development has the potential to impact upon a number of areas, not least development of personality, expression of intentions/emotions, perception of self and others and moral reasoning (Flavell 1985). In addition, when considering an individual young person's competence to consent, practitioners and researchers must be aware not only of his cognitive capacities, but also of his way of relating, and his networks with significant others. Sutton (1997) suggests that this is important because the identity of the young person is located in a network of relationships, and his autonomy is still developing.

Much has been written about the issue of consent to *treatment* and the authors consider that this framework is appropriate for thinking about consent to participate in *research* (both invasive and non-invasive). As with medical procedures, consent must be obtained before any research process can be undertaken.

WHAT MIGHT AFFECT COMPETENCE?

There are a number of factors that may affect an individual young person's competency in relation to providing consent. Practitioners and researchers need to make a careful assessment of competency before deciding whether an individual should be considered for possible inclusion in a research process.

As described above, it will be necessary to get information about not only the young person's chronological age, but also his social and emotional age. Such information may come from the young person himself, and also his carers. Immediately it will be apparent that, unlike research with adults, young people are always located in a network of carers who can claim to be involved in their decision. In forensic settings, the young people are often located in a legal network of carers, and we discuss the problems this poses in more detail later.

A second major factor in the assessment of competence is education and learning ability. In forensic settings in particular, it is likely that the forensic researcher will be working with children who have come from socially, emotionally and economically deprived backgrounds. Such deprivation negatively affects both attendance at education and the ability to learn, so that children and young people may lack basic literacy skills. They may also suffer from undetected specific and global learning disabilities which may make it difficult for them to engage with others. For this group, the chronological age distinction about ability to provide consent becomes entangled with issues of cognitive capacity and developmental level. Another potentially relevant issue is any history of head trauma (with or without loss of consciousness) which may have affected subsequent neurological development.

In forensic settings, the third factor for consideration must be the mental state of the child, and the question of how mental disorder or mental distress might affect competence to consent. Researchers will want to consider the effects of mood disorder, acute psychosis and ordinary distress following separation from family and friends on the capacity to take in information and make decisions.

COMPLEXITIES OF ESTABLISHING A CONSENT TO RESEARCH FRAMEWORK

All these factors may affect the individual's ability to consider the costs/benefits of participation, and his capacity to make a decision about participation. How best, then, to obtain consent from a young person for research purposes?

Carney and Tait (1997) suggest that an advocacy model be utilised as the method of choice to assist young people in their decision making, rather than a guardianship model, which supposes that someone makes the choice on the young person's behalf.

The Royal College of Psychiatry produced practice guidelines pertaining to *treatment* decisions taken by and on behalf of young people experiencing mental distress (Shaw 1999). The document concluded that real challenges were faced by practitioners regarding young people who presented with mental health or behavioural problems, which were due to both internal and external conflicts. Awareness of these conflicts in turn placed the professional in the difficult position of trying to provide vital information to the young person (and his carers) in an non-coercive manner, which respected both the young person's internal world needs and the needs of his 'external' world. Again, it is recommended that, where possible, utilising an independent arbiter can assist negotiations. Where an intervention has to be undertaken against the young person's will, the practitioner still needs to try to provide 'limited choices' for the young person, in an attempt to preserve some sense of autonomy for him.

In order to model 'best practice', researchers should examine the evidence available relating to all aspects of gaining consent. Much of the available information still relates to treatment rather than 'pure' research. The consequence is that, for many researchers, the only guidelines regarding consent are those provided by their local ethical committees. Local and national ethical committees provide guidelines for the types of written information that must be provided for potential research participants in relation to consent; for example, sample documents pertaining to consent (direct and proxy) and assent. The protocol must include an information sheet which:

1. is set out in language that is non-medicalised i.e. easy to understand

2. outlines the purpose of the research

3. outlines the potential benefits/risks of participating

4. makes it clear that they may decide not to participate

5. makes it clear they have the option to withdraw consent at any time.

Where possible, it is advocated that all individuals (participants and, where required, their carers) have information that they hold for the duration of their participation in the research in order that any decision they may make is based upon informed choice free from coercion.

Few of these guidelines contain information about the involvement of children and young people who may well be able to consent. There is also little advice about obtaining consent in settings where research participants are detained, or how to deal with situations where the potential participant may have competence limitations. For example, in order to assess learning disability (as part of the capacity assessment), it is necessary to do a psychological assessment. Is this assessment itself part of the research? Furthermore, if there is no identified learning disability at the time of consent, but subsequent research testing reveals one, is consent still valid?

In what follows we draw on our experience of carrying out research in a forensic facility for young people, and the practical problems we encountered in fulfilling our ethical and legal duty to obtain consent.

RESEARCH CASE HISTORY

A study was undertaken to look at the assessment of mental health needs, psychiatric disorder and personality functioning of juveniles entering the secure care system. The research involved collecting data on the psychosocial needs of a sample of 100 consecutive admissions to secure care facilities in England. The main aim was to determine whether the mental health needs change following admission to secure care. To date the project has recruited 100 male adolescents aged 10 to 17 years.

Information and consent

The authors became aware during the course of the research that the original documentation designed to give information about the research to potential participants did not meet all the requirements of all the various institutions who had an interest. These included not only the ethics committees who had to approve the study, but also the different residential institutions. As a result, these documents had to be adapted considerably (and repeatedly) to comply with different requests, many of which conflicted with each other.

It became apparent that the process of constructing these consent forms is intensely complicated, and influenced by local social and political interests. However, as the forms became more complicated, so they became less appropriate for children and young people who might have literacy or comprehension difficulties. It seemed difficult to balance the need to provide good quality information with the need to provide information in a manner that could actually be useful to those who were most involved.

The researcher made considerable efforts to investigate the young person's level of understanding of the research prior to seeking consent to participation. First, appropriate information was sent out to all significant others concerned with the young person's care, so that this could be considered prior to the researcher arranging to meet the young person. Second, when the researcher met with a young person, there was a period of questioning about his understanding of the research, and some discussion about the level of control each individual would have over the process, should he consent to participate and be accepted. The young person was informed of his right to withdraw at any point, and to ask questions about any aspect of the research. Where audio information was being obtained, he had the right to stop the tape at any point he wished. All potential participants were informed that data obtained (both qualitative and quantitative) would be anonymised, thus protecting their identity. They were also informed that their decision to accept or decline to participate would not affect their subsequent care.

Ethics of selection: 1. The identity of researchers

Once the method for obtaining consent had been decided upon, the researcher had to consider how this might affect sample selection procedure and subsequent sample size. The researchers utilised an 'opt in' approach to increase the young person's capacity to make an informed choice. The process of recruitment had a 'built-in' procedure whereby a named professional at a unit passed potential interviewees' names to the researcher. As the researcher was 'highly visible' within the units there was an increased opportunity for the young people to approach the researcher directly in order to be considered for inclusion.

The researcher was conscious of the importance of both his availability and openness when discussing the research with a potential participant. It was equally beneficial to pass details about the project to individuals who had most contact with the young person, i.e. his carer(s). The researcher also became aware of how positive perceptions of both the research and the researcher could be passed on by 'word of mouth'.

This recruitment situation was different to research involving some sort of interventions. In our situation, the researcher was highly visible; by contrast, in treatment or other types of intervention trials, the researcher or practitioner is often invisible until the intervention begins. In some trials, the researcher may not be identified to the participating individual at all. Building relationships with personnel who have responsibility for the young person may enhance co-operation and facilitate feedback. However, it is also possible that it biases selection and recruitment in some way; it may also result in researchers being drawn into the politics of the organisation, which may cloud their judgement.

Ethics of selection: 2. The identity of participants

Most ethical guidelines about research practice emphasise the duties of the researcher to protect the privacy of the participants, and consent to participation usually includes consent to publication and dissemination of research data in an anonymous and unidentifiable form. Research with forensic populations may present the researcher with a dilemma about the inclusion or exclusion of people whose cases are considered 'high profile'.

Exclusion of cases on a non-random basis is a potential source of bias for research samples; in studies involving small numbers, or case-based histories, this is particularly true. Clearly, high-profile subjects could theoretically consent or refuse in the usual way; however, if they were systematically excluded then the sample might not include potential beneficiaries and could become unrepresentative. What we found was that in some cases potential participants were excluded not by their own wishes but by agencies charged with responsibility for them. The reasons for this seem to focus on the 'protection' of the subject; however, we experienced this as being isolating and patronising for the young person, who in some cases had already agreed to participate.

CONSENT DILEMMAS

Three case vignettes are presented to illustrate some of the dilemmas faced when considering consent. All three cases relate to 15-year-old residents in local authority establishments.

Case A

This young person had heard about the research from his peers and was eager to participate. Having approached the researcher directly, the young person asked to be considered and the process of informal discussion commenced. The researcher briefly explained the process of providing information and obtaining consent from all relevant parties. The first individuals contacted were the key worker and social worker to discuss the young person's wishes. Information packs were provided and all local authority personnel were happy for the young person to participate. Contact then had to be made with the young person's carers (who did not have full legal responsibility) as the young person was under an S25 care order. The young person had a negative relationship with his carers and did not want the researcher to discuss the issue with them. Without the involvement of the carers, the young person was unable to participate.

This case demonstrates how parents, or those with parental responsibility, may provide consent or refuse research participation on behalf of the child. Their decision may be based on different reasons: family interests, religious beliefs and social values (Ross-Trevor 1996). Their health choice for their child may be based on their perception of the best possible chance even if evidence dictates otherwise (Brykcynska 1989). What is not clear is to what extent carers have a duty to represent and acknowledge the choices of the child.

Where carers and child conflict over therapy or research participation, there may be the added difficulty that the carer in fact does not 'know' the child all that well, but may be only *in loco parentis*. This is often the case for children and young people in forensic settings. For some young people the Home Office had full 'parental' responsibility. This radically changed the approach utilised and entailed the researchers obtaining direct consent from an outside agency who had minimal personal knowledge of the particular young person but who subsequently had to make decisions based upon whether the research would be of benefit to the young person. Such decisions might easily err in terms of being overcautious, which could lead to a dismissal of the young person's wishes, or in terms of lack of involvement, which might then really fail to consider all the young person's interests.

When this situation occurred, we made attempts to establish the rationale for carers refusing in the face of the young person's agreement. However, this was often not forthcoming. We speculated that the agencies involved were more concerned about the agency's legal liability in relation to the child rather than concerns regarding the particular research or the child's individual wishes.

Case B

A 15-year-old resident in a local authority unit approached the researcher directly and asked to be considered. The process of informal discussion commenced. With this particular young person, full legal responsibility had been transferred to the local authority; carers' views could be sought but ultimately social services would be in the parental role. A meeting was held to discuss the young person's wishes with social services, who argued that consent would have to be sought from the Home Office, simply because this was a high-profile case (not because the Home Office had responsibility for the young person). Consent was refused.

Case B resembles Case A; but here the involvement of other adults in the young person's consent is based on some anxieties about public attention. One anxiety must have been that the young person would have been identifiable; even though there were systems in place to prevent this. The agencies may have been concerned about media, rather than public, attention, and how they might be perceived in relation to this high-profile case. It is difficult to gauge whether agencies always act in a similar manner where the participant is described as a 'high-profile' case, i.e. consideration of political pressures and possible decreased collaboration with research.

Whilst researchers have to provide detailed written information regarding issues such as informed consent, researchers are often not provided with written information regarding proxy refusal of consent. The authors postulate that an individual's level of power is limited in institutions (regardless of whether he is an adolescent or an adult), so that agencies may perceive potential research subjects as particularly vulnerable (which they may well be). Research procedures are seen as exploitative because the subjects are detained, may be ill, and are vulnerable to inducements because they are deprived of liberty and possessions. Agencies may also be aware that researchers have other interests apart from the subjects; the research project is also a focus of their concern. However, it is also possible that, where properly and sensitively conducted, research participation can provide individuals with a sense of autonomy and empowerment.

Another explanation for this conflict is that agencies operate in a paternalistic manner, wanting to 'own' the young person and sometimes forgetting that the young person is the centre of the consent process which aims to respect his autonomy. It is difficult to gauge whether research undertaken in an adult facility would have met with the same response from agencies.

Case C

Following initial contact and discussion about the aims of the project, the young person agreed to participate. Contact was made with the key worker and the carers who had joint parental responsibility with the local authority. Although the carer and the young person consented, the local authority refused to give consent.

This case raises the question: do young people have a voice at all times? And how is this voice heard? We observed that there were occasions where the young persons' voice was not heard and their views not respected – this time on the grounds that he was under some stress or pressure, and therefore was not competent to consent.

In such cases the young person may have agreed to participate but the decision was taken out of his control. This type of scenario presents the researchers with a dilemma in that respect for the autonomy of the research subject is one of their primary ethical concerns. Where an individual's right to decide is withdrawn by external agencies, some rationale needs to be provided – not so much to the researchers but to the subjects whose view is being overridden. Similarly, the authors suggest that guidelines should be available to agencies and carers to assist the decision making process about whether a young person previously deemed not able to consent (due to illness or stress) is then able to consent. Guidelines, the authors suggest, could incorporate evidence regarding the effect of mental distress on competence to consent, which to date does not indicate that mild to moderate degrees of distress impair competence.

DISCUSSION

For any researcher, problems in obtaining consent may be eased by clear communication of the aims and objectives of the research with all the relevant parties. When a young person is resident in an environment where he cannot solely take responsibility for providing consent, it seems that conflicts of ownership of the young person's consent are inevitable. This is a function of autonomy being a developmental task (as discussed by Sutton 1997), so that competence to do many tasks will be an emerging and fluctuating state rather than a fixed state. The forensic nature of the settings seems to result in yet more agencies being involved who may take decisions which are based on third party interests, rather than those of the young person himself.

Consent and refusal rates have a direct influence on the nature and size of a sample, and the inferences that can then be drawn. It is possible that if the consent of young people is subject to too much external control, this will affect the knowledge base, and a gap will appear that could, in the longer term, negatively affect service development.

Where research involves examining delicate issues, all researchers have to balance the 'needs' of the individual against the needs of the young person's environment. On the whole the majority of the young people who participated in the authors' research were able to do so with few problems. Participation in the research was primarily related to the young person's legal status and secondly to the individual's care status. It is difficult for the authors to postulate whether the participation would have increased had the research only incorporated a community sample (thereby removing many of the legal restrictions on participants) or whether the participation rate was a genuine reflection of sampling. It would also have been interesting to establish whether the same barriers would have existed had the research examined physical rather than mental health needs.

For the majority of young people the issue of providing consent did not relate to anything the young people might gain in relation to their immediate need. Once they started the assessment the young people often provided rich verbal data that was extraneous to what was required (and in the main not recorded) but that enabled them the opportunity to 'open up' about some painful issues. The researcher had consistently informed the young people that anything they said that indicated they might be a danger to themselves or others would have to be discussed with their key worker. All of the young people accepted this clause. The duty of responsibility for all researchers (regardless of the age of the participants in their study or their capacity and competence to consent) must be to uphold the safety of the participant and others.

Mental health research typically deals with highly emotive issues, and researchers need to reflect on how such information is collected. If the information is of a sensitive nature, it is possible that staff and carers involved with the young person will also be uncomfortable with the same issues and, on the basis of their feelings, assume that the young person does not have the capacity to deal with issues. Researchers in this study sometimes observed that the young person valued the fact that the issue was not being avoided, but rather, for the first time, they were being asked direct questions. The research highlighted how much external agencies (regardless of whether they are official agencies or the carers) can take away the responsibility for a young person's ability to deal with uncomfortable issues.

The authors acknowledge that there are issues that have not been examined here, not least the differential relationship between the researcher and the participant. Who holds the perceived 'power': the person asking the questions or the person who is being asked the questions? Researchers also need to be able to identify the potential emotional impact for the participant, which may require some degree of empathic response from the researcher, as opposed to the complete detachment that is thought to be part of the scientific method traditionally. This may indeed be a particular isssue when working with young people whose emotional capacities are still in development and who therefore have greater dependency needs.

Similarly, researchers need to be conscious of theories that influence how questions are framed and information sought, and question how and whether their methodologies are gender and culture sensitive. More information is available regarding the impact of gender sensitivity – for example, the use of appropriate language at all stages. It is also true that oversensitivity can result in overgeneralisation (where studies deal with one sex but present themselves as being generally applicable) and sexual dichotomism (treating the sexes as two distinct groups rather than as groups who have overlapping characteristics) (Eichler 1988). Culture sensitivity requires the researcher to consider the 'needs' of the individual, and the social system in which the individual is located. Researchers are often unaware of their own and the participants' 'hidden assumptions' about culture and identity. Identity is an area that requires sensitive investigation; for example, an individual may display uncertainty about his cultural identity and may struggle to adapt to the culture of his peers rather than his family of origin. The language used must consider the identity of participants but not be perceived to be too distinctive or encourage oversensitivity. In this case, it may be that we needed more information about the institutional culture in which the staff and carers were working and living, in order to understand how the ethical conflicts arose.

CONCLUSION

Where research involves young people, there must be safeguards in relation to obtaining consent in order to protect the welfare and dignity of the participants. Practitioners and researchers need to be aware of their perceived position of power and exercise caution when informing interested parties about the costs/benefits of participation. They also need to consider the gender and cultural identity of the population under investigation and utilise appropriate language and methodology. Finally practitioners must consider the impact of participation on the overall physical and mental wellbeing of participants, and the networks of carers who are involved with them. Young people's identities are emerging as they grow and, as our research has shown, this has profound implications for participation in research.

REFERENCES

Booth, B. (1994) 'A Guiding Act?' *Nursing Times 90*, 8, 21–23.

Brykcynska, G. (1989) 'Informed Consent.' *Paediatric Nursing*, 6–8.

Carney, T. and Tait, D. (1997) 'Caught Between Two Systems? Guardianship and Young People with a Disability.' *Int Journal Law Psychiatry, 20*, 141–166.

Department of Health (1989) *The Children Act.* London: The Stationery Office.

Dickenson, D. (1994) 'Children's Informed Consent to Treatment. Is the Law an Ass?' *Journal of Medical Ethics, 20*, 205–206.

Eichler, M. (1988) 'The Double Standard: A Feminist Critique of Feminist Social Science.' In C. Robson (ed) (1993) *Real World Research; A Resource for Social Scientist and Practitioner Researcher.* Oxford: Blackwell, 63.

Flavell, J. H. (1985) *Cognitive Development* (2nd ed.) Englewood Cliffs, NJ: Prentice Hall.

HMSO (1983) *Mental Health Act.* London: The Stationery Office.

Ross-Trevor, J. (1996) 'Informed Consent and the Treatment of Children.' *Nursing Standard 10*, 50, 46–48.

Shaw, M. (1999) *Treatment Decisions in Young People (2) 'Practice Guidelines.'* The Focus Project. London: The Royal College of Psychiatrists Research Unit.

Sutton, A. (1997) 'Authority, Autonomy, Responsibility and Authorisation with Specific Reference to Adolescent Mental Health Practice.' *Journal of Medical Ethics*, 23, 26–31.

Trudeau, M. E. (1993) 'Informed Consent: The Patient's Right to Decide.' *Journal of Psychosocial Nursing, 31*, 6, 9–12.

CASES

'*Gillick* v. *West Norfolk and Wisbech Area Health Authority*' [1985] 3 All ER 402.

CHAPTER 3

Dangerous Stories

Consent and Confidentiality in Health and Social Care Research

Christine Brown

Traditional biomedical ethics falls short of encompassing ethical issues raised by the complete spectrum of health and social care research. In order to make an accurate assessment of potential risks and benefits to research participants, it is important to address this, otherwise potential for harm may be overlooked. As an example, a qualitative study on forensic patients suffering from personality disorder is considered. This study demonstrated two areas where special consideration of ethical issues was necessary: consent to the research process and dissemination of research findings. Health and social care research requires a broader perspective on ethical issues than that considered by biomedical research.

RESEARCHING HEALTH AND SOCIAL CARE

Medical research ethics has primarily been concerned with the effect of bio-medical research on patients. However, with the closer integration of health and social care in Britain today and the rise of the evidence-based model of clinical practice, evaluation of health services has become increasingly important. Research methods in health care have become progressively more eclectic in order to answer specific questions. Health services research has been defined as 'the integration of epidemiological, sociological, economic, and other analytic sciences in the study of health services' (Last 1988, p.58).

Traditional biomedical ethics makes the assumption that research subjects are passive rather than active participants in the scientific process. The patient has the research 'done to' him by the researcher. This follows the paradigm of biomedical research where investigations and interventions are focused on the biological functions or malfunctions of individuals, which are not owned by them, but become the property of the professional. In studies testing the effectiveness of new drugs, treatments or procedures, the choice facing subjects is whether to enter into the trial or not; after this, subsequent events are directed by the researcher's protocol which subjects consent to follow.

In health and social care research, methods often involve activities that are 'done with' the subject (questionnaire responses, focus groups, semi-structured or in-depth interviews). The active engagement of the individual, through his responses to questions, expressed opinions or related experiences, is an essential ingredient of such methods. Active service-user participation throughout the research process (Consumers in NHS Research Support Unit 2000) has become an integral part of NHS research and development policy.

The application of ethical reasoning based on models of relationships evolved from biomedical sciences can lead to problems when both the subject and researcher are engaged in health and social care research which is based on a different model of professional–participant relating.

Study example

This research project included qualitative data collected in the form of in-depth life history interviews with patients diagnosed as suffering from personality disorder in community and hospital settings and corresponding semi-structured interviews with professionals from different agencies (health services and criminal justice systems) involved in their care. The purpose was to examine explanatory models of personality disorder from different perspectives and assess their impact on pathways to care. This project raised several ethical issues relating to consent, confidentiality and dissemination of the results of research.

CONSENT IN MENTAL HEALTH RESEARCH

Issues of consent in mental health research often focus on whether the participants have the capacity to freely consent or whether their mental disorder limits that capacity to an unacceptable degree. Criteria for the assessment of capacity to consent to *treatment* are given by case law (*Re C* 1994). A patient is competent to give consent if he is able to understand and retain information, to believe information and to weigh information in balance and arrive at a decision. If a competent patient refuses treatment, that decision must be respected.

However, patients suffering from mental disorders may have their refusal of treatment overridden by law under the terms set out in the 1983 Mental Health Act (MHA). They are deemed to lack the capacity to give valid consent or refusal of consent to treatment. It is also possible for competent patients to be detained under the MHA as detention and treatment rests on the diagnosis of a disorder and not the patient's ability to make choices for himself. Most patients in psychiatric hospitals retain their capacity to make treatment choices, and involuntary treatment is in the minority of therapy offered.

In relation to research, psychiatric patients are no different to other health service users. Non-detained (informal) patients may be involved in research if they give consent to participate in a study. Guidance from the Mental Health Act Commission states that detained patients should not be prevented from participating in research if they have the capacity to consent (Mental Health Act Commission 1997). There is evidence to suggest that many psychiatric patients are able to understand the nature and purpose of research and can choose to participate (Appelbaum *et al.* 1999; Carpenter *et al.* 2000; Pinals *et al.* 1997).

Psychiatric patients who lack capacity to make health care decisions may be involved in research which causes minimal burden to them, and where the balance of risks and benefits has been approved by a Local Research Ethics Committee (LREC) (Royal College of Psychiatrists 2001). It is also a matter of good practice to obtain consent from a carer or advocate.

Capacity to consent and personality disorder

The capacity of patients suffering solely from personality disorder to give or withhold consent to treatment is a contentious issue in psychiatry. In clinical practice, patients with this diagnosis are often perceived as being competent to control their actions and so able to assume legal responsibility for them (Lewis and Appleby 1988). However, in criminal law, defendants with personality disorder have successfully claimed that the presence of the disorder has reduced their capacity to make decisions, and therefore 'impaired' their criminal responsibility (*Martin* v. *R.* 2001). The Mental Health Act 1983 makes a distinction between detention under the category of mental illness and detention under the category of psychopathic disorder, which is used in clinical practice to detain patients suffering solely from personality disorder. However, this 'persistent disorder or disability of mind' is only recognised by law in cases where 'abnormally aggressive or seriously irresponsible conduct' result. A White Paper has proposed the abolition of this distinction between mental illness and psychopathic disorder, to be replaced with the term mental disorder, defined as 'any disability or disorder of mind or brain, whether permanent or temporary, which results in an impairment of mental functioning' (Reforming the Mental Health Act 2000).

Under the 1983 MHA, detention by the legal category of psychopathic disorder also requires that the would-be patient is 'treatable' i.e. that 'treatment is likely to alleviate or prevent a deterioration in their condition' (*R. v. Cannons Park MHRT* 1994). There is no such requirement for patients with mental illness. In a recent study of 'treatability' decisions in a sample of forensic patients, the most significant differentiating factor identified by clinicians was evidence of motivation to engage in treatment (i.e. a wish for treatment), genuineness and understanding (Berry, Duggan and Larkin 1999). If the criteria for treatability are linked to 'genuine' motivation and understanding, it seems likely that patients detained under the MHA category of psychopathic disorder will retain capacity to consent to treatment.

However, the relationship between the *legal* category of psychopathic disorder and the *medical* classification of personality disorders is not straightforward. Personality disorders that do not result in abnormally aggressive or seriously irresponsible conduct (which are the majority) will not be equivalent to the legal notion of psychopathic disorder. Many people with personality disorders may suffer psychological symptoms which might impair decision making processes such as impulsivity, transient psychotic symptoms and affective instability. The impact on decision making capacity in patients with different clusters of personality disorders has not been systematically studied, for either consent to treatment or research procedures. However, given that patients with other types of mental illness can retain decision making capacity, it seems reasonable to suppose that this will also be true for personality disorder.

CONSENT PROCEDURES

The discussion thus far on capacity of consent in people suffering from personality disorder applies equally to any proposed research. However, it is in the procedures for obtaining consent that differences arise between the ethical implications of different types of research methods.

Biomedical research ethics guidelines focus on the one-stage process of obtaining consent. It is the researcher's duty to inform each subject of:

> the aims, methods, sources of funding, any possible conflicts of interest, institutional affiliations of the researcher, the anticipated benefits and potential risks of the study and the discomfort it may entail... After ensuring that the subject has understood the information, the physician should then obtain the subjects' freely-given informed consent, preferably in writing. (World Medical Association 2000)

This advice is straightforward when the decision to participate in research involves the patient in a one-stage process. The decision is either to take a chance and receive an experimental treatment or not. Once the patient is entered into the trial, he may change his mind, withdraw consent and drop out but he will have already received some part of the treatment. This irreversible, one-way process of biomedical research is reflected in the analysis of results that take into account and draw conclusions from the drop-out rates of entered subjects in the study.

In health and social care research, data collection can entail an ongoing active engagement between the researcher and participant. When using qualitative research methods, data analysis runs concurrently with data collection (Brown and Lloyd 2001). Iterative data analysis guides further purposive sampling and data collection, thus the research agenda may shift according to the emergent themes. Though it is possible at the beginning of the research to outline proposed areas of inquiry and any expected problematic issues that may arise, it is difficult to precisely predict final outcomes. In these circumstances, a one-stage consent model signed on entry into the study is misleading to researcher and participant alike. It may be preferable to include an ongoing consent protocol, or to gain additional written consent once data collection is completed.

The fact that qualitative methods provoke particular ethical issues with consent of research subjects has been acknowledged in the social science literature (Reynolds 1982). Debate has largely focused on the use of covert research and whether there are any acceptable degrees of deception permissible as part of the research process. This was provoked by high-profile studies such as Milgram's research in social psychology, where participants were led to believe that they were inflicting pain on another person as part of a laboratory experiment (Milgram 1963). The current position on covert observation in social science is summed up by Bulmer as harmful to subjects, researchers and the academic discipline espousing such methods (Bulmer 1982). However, although uncomfortable with outright deception, those engaged in participant observation research or fieldwork have argued that it is practically impossible to obtain formal written consent from all people who interact with the researcher and theoretically problematic as this prevents events from unfolding in their usual way (Weppner 1977). Others engaged in research with marginal groups such as criminals argue that formal written consent significantly reduces participation and this prevents the collection of valuable data (Klockars and O'Connor 1979). In the USA, it is possible for research ethics review boards to grant fieldwork studies a waiver of informed consent (Penslar 1993).

This again demonstrates the importance of strict attention to the details of methodology when considering potential risks and benefits of research. Just because a study uses qualitative data and an analytic framework from the social sciences, it does *not* automatically follow that the researcher should argue for a waiver of informed consent. In studies using in-depth interviews, the relationship between the subject and researcher has been described as developing over the course of data collection 'from sympathetic observer, through sounding board to confessor and emotional prop' (Faraday and Plummer 1979, p.789). This in turn affects the material disclosed by the subject to the researcher. The resulting 'research friendships' (Faraday and Plummer 1979, p.791) pose questions of frank exploitation of the subject by the researcher. On completion of data collection, the withdrawal of this relationship can leave subjects feeling angry and betrayed (Punch 1989, 1998). This makes the renewal of consent at the end of the data collection process (preferably after a subsequent cooling off or disengagement period for the subject) even more important from the point of view of both participant and researcher.

ETHICAL ISSUES OF CONSENT IN THE STUDY EXAMPLE

The study example demonstrated the difficulties with a one-stage consent process when utilising this particular methodology. In-depth interviews use few predetermined themes and aim to follow the subject's emerging narrative account. They are long, usually four to six hours staged over two or three meetings, tape-recorded and subsequently transcribed verbatim. The life-history interview aims to facilitate the subject's description in chrono-logical order of significant events leading up to the present, to give a 'retro-spective account by the individual of his life…that has been elicited or prompted by another person' (Watson and Watson-Franke 1985, p.2). This technique has been used predominantly in social sciences, though has origins in psychology and psychiatry (Allport 1942, Freud 1991).

The use of life-history interviews in this particular study population raised ethical concerns regarding capacity and consent. Patients suffering from personality disorder experience difficulties with interpersonal rela-tionships, such as intense attachments or fear of abandonment. The interview process itself engaged the researcher and participant in a relation-ship where such dynamics might be acted out. Indeed, there was more than a passing resemblance to the structure of the life-history interview and a psychotherapy assessment interview. There was a risk that such patients may be particularly vulnerable to exploitation as their dependency needs and attachments may make it difficult for them to say no, abuse histories may make them hypersensitive to power imbalances and the likely occurrence of dissociative states may affect capacity to give valid consent. Provocation of traumatic memories was likely to result from the interview process. It was important that the participant understood these risks prior to entering the study, that good communication was maintained between the researcher and the clinical team and that support was ongoing for the participant after each interview episode.

The assessment of a participant's capacity to give consent was made by the patient's clinical team. This was reviewed by the participant's key worker prior to each episode of researcher contact. When the participant was resident on an in-patient ward, this system worked well, but practical problems were encountered with participants living in the community. Consent was recorded in writing at entry into the study on three separate forms, as stipulated by the Multi-centre Research Ethics Committee: one consent to participate in the research project, one consent for the researcher to contact named professionals for semi-structured interviews and one consent for the interview to be audiotaped. Once the interviews were completed and transcribed, the researcher met with the participant again to read through the transcribed document. At this meeting, participants were able to make any changes to the document either by adding to or cutting out parts of the text. This was also used as an opportunity to review consent to participate in the research.

Confidentiality and dissemination of results

Reviewing consent at the end of the data collection process allowed the participant to focus more clearly on issues of what would happen to the research data – that is, where the transcripts would be kept, who would read them, what the data analysis would involve, how the results of the research might be presented and disseminated.

The final review of the transcript with the participants marked the end of their contact with the researcher. They were asked to reaffirm their consent that the document could be taken away and used for the purposes of the research. In doing this, assurances were given that no-one would read the document other than the researcher, that it would be stored in a secure place and that their confidentiality was assured in the publication of any material resulting from the research. This is possible because interview transcripts are the raw data from which relevant general stable themes are derived. For the purposes of this study, it was agreed that in certain settings themes derived from the research interviews would be first outlined to the individual's clinical team in order to ensure that confidentiality was not inadvertently breached. In the presentation of results of qualitative data derived from interviews, it is common to use brief quotes to illustrate points, as long as these do not allow retrospective identification of participants. Key individual signifiers, such as age, gender or setting, might be adapted in published material in order to preserve participant anonymity; however, this has to be carefully balanced against the context of the quote so that the interpretive meaning is not altered.

However, there is an inherent assumption here that participants desire anonymity in the research process. Due to the personal nature of the data collected, it is possible that some participants may be motivated by the very fact that the research offers the chance to tell their own story. By participating in a research study, participants may expect particular attention to be paid to their personal experiences and may not be adverse to these reaching the public domain. If the participants are judged as competent to give consent to research participation, would the researcher be justified in using identifiable material in the presentation of results if the participant explicitly gave his consent?

My view is that for researchers studying in forensic settings, the answer is no. Life events do not happen to individuals in isolation but to people existing in a complex network of relationships. The right to confidentiality of other people involved in participants' lives, be they carers, victims or professionals, also needs to be considered in the presentation of this type of research. The potential for harm caused by the research must include this network of relationships as well as the relationship between participant and researcher. Therefore, in forensic mental health research, consent for publication of a case report does not rest solely with the individual subject as is the case in biomedical research.

There is evidence from social science studies that disclosure by researchers of intimate details of participants' daily lives, even with their express consent, may result in harm both to participants and others (Bulmer 1982; Kimmel 1988; Reiss 1979). These may not emerge until many years after publication (Boelen 1992; Whyte 1943, 1992). Such risks of harm are problematic as they remain largely unknowable, in much the same way that long-term side-effects of newly marketed medications are always possible. The role of the researcher is to attend to the minimisation of potential risks, and the ethical review body to judge whether these risks are justified.

Ownership of data

In social science disciplines, accepted practice is that the ownership of a life-history narrative lies with the person who lives that narrative and tells his story (Atkinson 1998). Life histories are seen to be the property of the person from whom the data has been elicited, as prior to the research process in the form of the in-depth interview the life-history narrative was not in the public domain. From this perspective, the researcher and subject are in a collaborative project and each have rights as co-authors of resulting data. Publication involves negotiation of copyright with the research participant, who is entitled to a share of royalties and editorial rights over the material published.

However, forensic mental health research raises ethical issues of third party confidentiality, often compounded by the fact that third parties are victims of offences perpetrated by research participants. In England, an insight into the dominant moral discourse surrounding offenders was demonstrated by the public debate provoked by payment to an offender on publication of her biography (Sereny 1998). This was predominantly condemned as profiteering from crime. The principle that research participants in this study should receive payment or share editorial control over published material was overridden by the principle of protection from harm of third parties.

In the study example, different research ethics committees found different points of balance between research participants' rights and third party rights. The researchers believed that a recognition of participants' collaborative role in the interview process was important despite the limitations outlined above. The protocol stated that following final editing with the researcher of the interview transcript, the participant would also receive a copy of the document. The participant information sheet suggested that this document might be used in a psychotherapeutic session or shared with the medical team; however, participants would be able to choose to do whatever they wished with the transcript. On ethical review, some committees felt that this would place the confidentiality of other individuals at too great a risk. It was argued that there was a potential for harm to third parties – for instance, if the participant posted the document to a journalist requesting publication. The participants had the potential to tell dangerous stories. This overrode their right to own those stories and to choose when to tell them. Thus in forensic mental health services settings, research participants themselves were viewed as a source of potential harm, with corresponding restrictions on their rights to freedom of expression. Where this leaves the participant-focused principles of biomedical ethics is unclear.

CONCLUSION

The closer integration of health and social care also juxtaposes interdisciplinary research methodologies which may require a reappraisal of biomedical-focused research ethics. Health and social care research can raise particular ethical issues which the application of assumptions from biomedical sciences may overlook. For example, in the use of narrative-based research (Greenhalgh and Hurwitz 1998), it is important to remember that individual narratives do not exist in isolation but are always situated in a context of time, place and social network.

REFERENCES

Allport, G. (1942) *The Use of Personal Documents in Psychological Science.* New York: Social Science Research Council.

Appelbaum, P., Grisso, T., Ellen, F., O'Donnell, S. and Kupfer, D.J. (1999) 'Competence of Depressed Patients to Consent to Research.' *American Journal of Psychiatry,* 156, 1380–1384.

Atkinson, R. (1998) *The Life Story Interview.* Sage University Papers Series on Qualitative Research Methods, Vol. 44. Thousand Oaks, CA: Sage.

Berry, A., Duggan, C. and Larkin, E. (1999) 'The Treatability of Psychopathic Disorder: How Clinicians Decide.' *Journal of Forensic Psychiatry,* 10, 710–719.

Boelen, W.A.M. (1992) 'Street Corner Society: Cornerville Revisited.' *Journal of Contemporary Ethnography 21,* 11–51.

Brown, C. S. H. and Lloyd, K. (2001) 'Qualitative Methods in Psychiatric Research.' *Advances in Psychiatric Treatment 7,* 4, 350–356.

Bulmer, M. (ed) (1982) *Social Research Ethics.* London: Macmillan.

Carpenter, W., Gold, L., Lahti, A., Queern, C., Conley, R., Bartko, J., Kovnick, J. and Appelbaum, P. (2000) 'Decisional Capacity for Informed Consent in Schizophrenia Research.' *Arch Gen Psych 57,* 533–538.

Consumers in NHS Research Support Unit (2000) *Involving Consumers in Research and Development in the NHS: Briefing Notes for Researchers.* Eastleigh: Consumers in NHS Research Support Unit.

Department of Health (1983) Mental Health Act. London: HMSO.

Department of Health (2000) Reforming the Mental Health Act. London: TSO.

Faraday, F. and Plummer, K. (1979) 'Doing Life Histories.' *Sociological Review,* 27, 773–798.

Freud, S. (1991) *Introductory Lectures on Psychoanalysis.* London: Penguin.

Greenhalgh, T. and Hurwitz, B. (1998) *Narrative Based Medicine.* London: BMJ Books.

Kimmel, A. (1988) *Ethics and Values in Applied Social Research.* Newbury Park: Sage.

Klockars, C.B. and O'Connor, F.W. (eds) (1979) *Deviance and Decency: The Ethics of Research with Human Subjects.* Beverley Hills, CA: Sage.

Last, J.M. (ed) (1988) *A Dictionary of Epidemiology* (2nd edition). New York: Oxford University Press.

Lewis, G. and Appleby, L. (1988) 'Personality Disorder: The Patients Psychiatrists Dislike.' *British Journal of Psychiatry,* 153, 44–49.

Mental Health Act Commission (1997) *Position Paper 1: Research Involving Detained Patients.* Nottingham: Mental Health Act Commission.

Milgram, S. (1963) 'Behavioural Study of Obedience.' *Journal of Abnormal and Social Psychology,* 67, 371–378.

Penslar, R. L. (1993) *Protecting Human Research Subjects: Institutional Review Board Guidebook.* (2nd edition). Washington, DC: US Department of Health and Human Services, Public Health Service, National Institutes of Health, Office of Extramural Research, Office for Protection from Research Risks.

Pinals, D., Malhotra, A.K., Breier, A. and Pickar, D. (1997) 'Informed Consent in Schizophrenia Research.' *Psychiatric Services 49,* 244.

Punch, M. (1989) 'Researching Police Deviance: A Personal Encounter with the Limitations and Liabilities of Fieldwork.' *British Journal of Sociology,* 40, 177–204.

Punch, M. (1998) 'Politics and Ethics in Qualitative Research.' In N. Denzin and Y. Lincoln (eds) *The Landscape of Qualitative Research: Theories and Issues.* London: Sage.

Reiss, A. (1979) 'Government Regulation in Scientific Inquiry: Some Paradoxical Consequences.' In C. B. Klockars and F. W. O'Connor (eds) (1979) *Deviance and Decency: The Ethics of Research with Human Subjects.* Beverly Hills, CA: Sage.

Reynolds, P. (1982) *Ethics and Social Science Research.* NJ: Prentice-Hall.

Royal College of Psychiatrists (2001) 'Guidelines for Researchers and for Research Ethics Committees on Psychiatric Research Involving Human Participants.' *Council Report: CR82.* London: Gaskell.

Sereny, G. (1998) *Cries Unheard: The Story of Mary Bell.* London: Macmillan.

Watson, C.W. and Watson-Franke, M.B. (1985) *Interpreting Life Histories: Life History Research in Anthropology.* Rutgers University Press: New Jersey.

Weppner, R.S. (1977) *Street Ethnography.* Beverley Hills, CA: Sage.

Whyte, W.F. (1943) *Street Corner Society: The Social Structure of an Italian Slum.* Chicago: University of Chicago Press.

Whyte, W.F. (1992) 'In Defense of Street Corner Society.' *Journal of Contemporary Ethnography 21,* 52–68.

World Medical Association (1964, amended Tokyo 1975, Venice 1983, Hong Kong 1989, South Africa 1996 and Edinburgh 2000) *Declaration of Helsinki: Recommendations Guiding Physicians in Biomedical Research Involving Human Subjects.* Helsinki: World Medical Association.

CASES

Martin v. *R.* [2001] EWCA Crim 2245.

Re C (Adult: Refusal of Medical Treatment) [1994] 1 All ER 819.

R. v. *Cannons Park MHRT,* ex parte A [1994].

CHAPTER 4

User Views and Ethical Issues in Qualitative Methods

Annie Bartlett and Krysia Canvin

INTRODUCTION

Qualitative methods are increasingly often used in research on patient populations. Despite this, many medical researchers are unfamiliar with both the scope and detail of qualitative techniques and ignorant of the kinds of knowledge generated by this research.[1] This chapter will examine the ethical issues specific to a range of qualitative techniques used in health services research with forensic populations. It will illustrate key points using material from three qualitative projects: interview studies of women prisoners, staff and patients in medium secure units, and mental health system patients living under compulsory orders in the community.[2]

The chapter is particularly concerned to explore the lack of autonomy consequent on detention of those with or without mental disorder and the necessity of detailed findings specific to qualitative work. We argue that the detail intrinsic to such work confronts researchers in forensic settings with ethical dilemmas stemming from the sensitivity of research information and the possible identification of research participants.

ACCESS TO PARTICIPANTS AND CAPACITY TO PARTICIPATE[3]

Patient or prisoner participants in forensic research are far from autonomous. This raises important questions for both qualitative and quantitative researchers about access to institutions and individuals, and the capacity of individuals to consent to research. Researching any sample of prisoners or hospitalised patients is ethically problematic, in view of the fact that they are a captive study population (quite literally). This raises doubts as to whether they are able to give true, voluntary, informed consent. There is always the real or perceived risk that undue pressure may be brought to bear on prisoners/patients to participate in research or not to withdraw from it. There is, therefore, a need to ensure that free consent is being exercised and that as full information as is possible is provided to inform this consent. It is worthwhile rehearsing these issues before explaining how they connect specifically to qualitative philosophy of inquiry and technique.

Prisoners and hospitalised patients are vulnerable because of their lack of resources and personal autonomy. Roberts argues that women generally are chosen as respondents for research because they are willing to act as such: 'because they are less willing to slam the door on the researcher, more likely than are men to be socialised to want to be helpful, and because they are perceived as being more flexible in relation to demands on their time' (Roberts 1992, p.180). As such it is imperative that potential participants are not exploited, that participation is wholly voluntary and ideally that they derive some benefit from the research.

Gatekeeping of the mentally disordered

An element of gatekeeping is expected in all research where a body of people or an individual is invested with the power to grant or refuse access to the chosen research population. This gatekeeping role intensifies where the study population is vulnerable or lacking in autonomy, where health care is provided or restrictions on freedom imposed. In some situations, gatekeeping may even be perceived as desirable.

We encountered gatekeeping by the key workers (community psychiatric nurses or social workers) of mental health service users subject to compulsory supervision in the community. Contact with the mental health service users was attempted through the key worker, in view of privacy and safety considerations and in the absence of a suitable alternative. Not all key workers agreed to allow the researcher to access the selected service user. In this instance, the gatekeeping was paternalistic and protective, revealing concern that approaching service users could cause 'too much distress'. Here, the relationship between a potential participant's status and his loss of autonomy was demonstrated. Key workers were reluctant to give access to service users they felt were 'not well enough', despite permission having been granted by the Responsible Medical Officer and the approval of the relevant ethics committee. The mental health status of the potential participants was a key factor in key workers' decisions to refuse access, although they were describing common features of mental illness, 'visual and auditory hallucinations', 'difficult to engage, easily distracted', or side-effects from the medication, 'not coherent because drugged'. Concern was also expressed by key workers about the capacity of individuals to 'take in simple information', to 'have any understanding of the context of the interview', or to return 'much information'. The application of such criteria to determine capacity would serve to exclude all persons exhibiting mental health problems from participation in research.

The concept of 'capacity' is used to determine whether someone is autonomous and whether he can be legally responsible. The law presumes capacity unless there is evidence to the contrary. In the context of medical treatment, a three stage test exists to determine capacity: a person must be capable of: 1. comprehending and retaining relevant treatment information, 2. believing it, and 3. weighing it in the balance to arrive at a choice (Re C 1994). On this basis, it has been established that people with mental illness, including illnesses that grossly disturb perceptions and beliefs, can retain the capacity to decide whether or not to accept treatment (Re C 1994). Guidelines suggest that capacity to consent to research is assessed in the same way as capacity to consent to treatment (Law Society and British Medical Association 1995). Research has ascertained that persons with schizophrenia are able to understand research consent forms (Carpenter et al. 2000) and can do so equally as well as persons without schizophrenia (Pinals et al. 1998). This has led to the recommendation that service users' decisions to participate in research should be respected (Hofman et al. 1999). We believe that this principle should be extended to include giving service users the opportunity to decide whether to participate in research. Researchers must build safeguards into their consent procedures to reassure both potential participants and gatekeepers. In this study all potential participants were given information about the study and a free choice whether to participate, including a cooling-off period of at least 24 hours between the giving of consent and the interview. In fact one potential participant was considered unable to understand the study and the role of the researcher, and was not interviewed.

In the study indicated above, the researchers' only practical route to participants was through professionals. The gatekeeping role of these professionals was particularly delicate, as it involved vulnerable participants who may have been easily influenced or distressed. In practice these professionals may have simply been silencing the people they were trying to protect. The research put the professionals in a position of power such that they could refuse access where they wished to stifle possible criticism of themselves, though we have no evidence that this happened. The wider ramifications of gatekeeping are that it then becomes difficult to obtain a representative picture of participant experiences. Participants may be denied both an opportunity to decide for themselves and to speak of their own experiences. For mental health service users this reinforces the idea that they are unable to provide a valid opinion about the mental health services they use (Rogers *et al.* 1993), and that it is legitimate not to encourage or support them in doing so. This is also at odds with recommendations from central government that lay people contribute in a more active way to the research process rather than simply being the 'passive objects of study' (Rogers *et al.* 1993).

Participants should have choice and control over the kind of research in which they participate. A minority of mental health service users or patients would be distressed or confused by involvement in research in any manner, and to attempt to include them would be inappropriate. Care should be taken when deciding whether to give potential participants and the professionals involved the choice whether to participate. Where this is done in conjunction with or on the advice of the professionals, their involvement in this process must be documented and assessed for its impact.

Gatekeeping of prisoners

Gatekeeping was also encountered in the study of pregnant women prisoners, but it operated differently. Despite efforts to minimise the role of prison staff (prison officers and governors) in the selection and recruitment of participants through the display of a poster to attract women to volunteer for the study, posters were not always displayed. Instead, potential participants were approached by members of staff weeks or days before the date of the researcher's visit, and sometimes on the same day. This threatened the prospect of obtaining voluntary informed consent, as well as potentially excluding willing volunteers (considered inappropriate or troublesome by prison staff). Prison staff justified the practice on the grounds that there were so few pregnant women they could be easily identified and located, then approached personally. Where this occurred, great care was taken by the interviewer to give potential participants in these circumstances the opportunity to refuse or to withdraw.

Even where attempts are made to circumvent gatekeeping, it may occur anyway. Also, gatekeeping may not only involve the prevention of access, but also the coerced participation of unwilling participants. Those detained in prison or hospital are a disempowered population and, as such, cannot avoid being approached in person to participate in research. They may also have less control over personal information, whether this is provided from records or orally by staff, without their permission.

The credibility of the patient/prisoner voice

Participants' voices can be undermined by their status as persons convicted of criminal offences and/or living with mental illness, based on the notion that they will be untruthful, or unable to give sensible answers. This is a significant issue in qualitative research because of its potential for high face validity, in contrast to the high reliability of quantitative research. Thus any study is required to reflect on validity using the intellectual arsenal of qualitative inquiry including reflexivity and the triangulation of data sources.

The key workers in the compulsory supervision study alluded to the idea that the service users would be unable to give meaningful responses, and researchers introduced to prisoners by prison staff are often warned not to believe everything that they are told. There is also suspicion that those aggrieved by their detention against their will in prison or hospital, or statutory restrictions on their freedom in the community, only consent to participate in a study with their own ulterior motive or agenda, perhaps to air a grievance. This issue was thoroughly explored in the two Ashworth Inquiries (1992, 1999) where the credibility of patient observation and experiences was evaluated, although not in a research context. In the first Ashworth Inquiry (1992, 15–21) particular care was taken to clarify criteria that would allow the contributions of detained forensic patients to be assessed. They consider the way in which particular mental health problems can affect the recording of events and the ability to describe it subsequently, as well as the personal and institutional factors that should be taken into account when weighing evidence. They acknowledge the possibility that the subjects of forensic research can be hostile to the aims of the institution controlling them. The guidance given here is particularly helpful for those doing qualitative research in a forensic setting, as many of the issues are the same.

Responsibility of the researcher

Researchers operating in health care settings have a range of disciplinary backgrounds and their previous activity may have been governed by the different ethical standards applying both within the discipline and within the setting.

There are a number of potential difficulties between the rules of health care research and the demands of particular disciplines, which have ethical dimensions. The first is the status of the access story that can form a necessary element of a qualitative account of health service research. The purpose of writing it is to provide necessary, personal and institutional context for the account – yet there will be no indication in the research protocol that this will be included in this way in writing up. Second, although interview- and documentary-based studies can comply with ethics committees' demands for written consent, observation-based studies have more difficulty. This is because in practice not everyone who walks into the space occupied by the researcher can easily and appropriately be fully informed about the research. This has long been recognised as an issue in disciplines where observation research is routine, but can take medical ethics committees by surprise. Third, the open-ended nature of qualitative research techniques can conflict with the constraints implicit in the duties of the ethics committees when they approve research without being able to know the end point of data collection. Fine judgements and considerable integrity is then required of the researchers in being true to the aims of the project while bearing in mind the academic standards of the discipline in which they are working. They are balancing the discovery of new ideas relevant to the intention of the study against the gratuitous questioning and observation of research subjects for no useful or approved purpose. One way in which qualitative researchers can check informants are happy with the material they have produced, although it is sometimes hard to do in practice, is respondent validation. This can work well for interview studies, where the interview material is shared with the informant before analysis, but has no obvious way of being applied in documentary- or observation-based work.

Not only can this compromise the research if respondents object to what they actually said, it also places an additional burden on participants.

THE REPRESENTATION OF PARTICIPANTS' VIEWS AND EXPERIENCES

Qualitative research provides authentic and detailed explanations of the people and settings studied, and the meanings, experiences and perceptions of those concerned. It is also open-ended in character. It may cover sensitive and private personal experience in considerable depth, perhaps in more detail than the person intended when he gave consent. There is potential for conflict with the ethical goals of confidentiality and anonymity for research participants. The duty for researchers is to balance the representation of data with the protection of participants' anonymity and confidentiality. Research cannot be ethically justified if the process of anonymising distorts rather than disguises, nor if researchers are cavalier about the confidentiality of material.

Identification of participants

Participants in any study face the risk that their identity could be discovered and their privacy compromised. To reduce this risk, various standard measures are easily taken in quantitative research to ensure that data collected is kept confidential and anonymous. In order to assure anonymity, researchers must store data in such a way that in the event of persons gaining access to the material without permission, measures taken would prevent the identification of any participants. Also, data should not be published or released in a form that would permit the actual or potential identification of participants.

Although these measures do transfer to qualitative research in terms of superficial anonymising of data and data storage, the problem comes in the writing-up stage of a project. Adhering rigidly to the principle of protecting the identity of participants in research can be easier in theory than in practice. The presentation of data is difficult, especially where small numbers are involved, and it is a truism of qualitative work that it sacrifices breadth to depth. There are situations where it is important to write about specific individuals in unusual and highly identifiable circumstances, a common scenario in the case study of an event or episode. Sometimes, it is vitally important to be able to refer to specific characteristics of a very small group of people who, whether discussed individually or collectively, would be easily identifiable to those around them. Aside from the obvious ethical dilemmas this raises in relation to confidentiality and anonymity for the individual participant, there are also the ramifications for family members and friends.

An overlooked issue in this area is that of degree of identification. Confidentiality is usually discussed as a binary phenomenon: you either preserve it or you breach it. This conceptualisation may owe something to discussion within a legal framework, in relation to clinical care. However, the truth of research anonymity, in the context of qualitative research, is that it is not an all-or-none phenomenon; it is a matter of degree. The apparent degree of anonymity will vary according to who is accessing the publication, and this is unavoidable.

The first variant of anonymity is institutional anonymity. Both interview and observational studies can be based in one or more institutions. Some researchers have disguised the location of their research (Peay 1989) and some have not (Cardoza-Freeman 1984; Davidson 1974). Possibly this is down to the vagaries of ethics committees or disciplinary affiliation. In practice it helps, but certainly does not ensure the anonymity of informants. Readers may guess the identity of an institution but they will not know it.

The second variant of anonymity is the time lapse between events and publication. Funding bodies are very keen to see short intervals between research and publication, presumably believing that this rush into print is more likely to increase the sum total of human knowledge than well-digested, thoughtful contributions published later. However, a time lag between research and publication may, usually inadvertently, make it harder both for those in the same place at the same time, and anyone else, to identify particular people or places. The human elements of events and institutions change. The people who constitute the wing of a prison move on.

The third variant of anonymity is that of personal identity. The sources of information (documentary, interview, observational material), whether they are public or private, and the area of research interest (events or individuals) will make a significant difference to the ease with which identification is minimised. Public events are harder to disguise than private confidences. Thus observational material is particularly easy to spot, if you have been involved, but naturally harder to pinpoint if you are outside the event. Therefore what may be known to staff and prisoners within a prison setting, e.g. who was involved in a violent incident or who runs the prison music group, whose performance was witnessed by researchers, is still unidentifiable to the casual reader. Information obtained in private can seem easier to anonymise. However, the regular use of quotation from private interviews (as opposed to verbatim presentation of conversation of public discussion) has its own hazards. People do remember what they say and extensive quotation could lead participants to identify their contribution if they were to read the publication.

A range of techniques exists to minimise the risk of unwanted identification. These include avoiding the use of unique identifiers in the presentation of data, such as the broad banding of personal characteristics (e.g. age, length of time detained), or the use of composite case studies. In both methods, grouping them together in such a way that only their collective personal characteristics and opinions are discussed reduces the likelihood of participants being identified. An alternative is to change the obvious identifying characteristics of individuals, e.g. names, ages, gender, role and social origin. For places the options are different. Modifications can easily be made to names and locations. However, editing, omitting or otherwise altering the history of the place or details of functions carries a considerable risk of unacceptable distortion.

Sensitivity of information

The concern with identification and confidentiality originates in an anxiety on the part of researchers about publicising information that participants in research wish to remain private.[4] The working assumption is that this is reasonable on the part of participants, though it is possible to imagine circumstances where it is more ethical to disclose such information than not to do so.

This working assumption leads us to consider several scenarios: first, where the information provided to researchers is personal, perhaps unknown to existing third parties, and delicate in nature; second, where the information relates to high-profile individuals whose personal details would lead to media interest; third, where event disclosure could lead to recriminations for the disclosing informant. The fact that such information has been given with consent does not provide the researcher with an automatic ethical alibi providing they change the name of the person concerned. These scenarios are more likely in qualitative research for two reasons, both because the research is relatively in-depth and because the open-ended nature of inquiry can lead people to say and do things that with hindsight they might have left unsaid and undone.

The second and third scenarios were relevant to a study of staff and patients in medium secure units where the issue examined was the quality of service provided to women patients. There are real dangers in investigating small, high-profile groups, such as women secure hospital patients or the women in Durham H block, whose future might be affected by unwanted publicity. Women patients in forensic settings are small in number (Hassell and Bartlett 2001). Heidensohn (1985) drew attention some time ago to the representation of women criminals and their mythologisation in the media. Women approached in this study showed an awareness of these issues.

Part of the study was to examine issues of safety and possible experiences of threat or assault. Such information can be very demanding to disclose and forces the researcher to consider in what circumstances, if any, the clinical team of the patient might be informed. The issue of recrimination in the event of identification is more likely to apply in settings where public access is restricted and where unwanted behaviours, e.g. bullying, physical and sexual violence, are common. This applies to forensic settings but not uniquely so. Because of the range of social and psychological phenomena likely to be explored in qualitative work, researchers need to think these issues through before they start collecting data. Participants may report events such as bullying or assault, which could place them in a vulnerable position in the institution, at risk of victimisation, which they decide they would rather not be publicised, even anonymously. Care subsequently needs to be taken in how such information is presented for publication, particularly in the context of tape-recorded interviews. The obverse of this is not publishing reckless allegations about host institutions without thoroughly exploring or qualifying the validity of such accounts through the routine checks and balances of qualitative data analysis.

Despite measures to protect anonymity and confidentiality, participants must be warned that, in spite of precautions, identification could be possible if a combination of attributes arose which could not be disguised without distorting the data and, as a result, *absolute* anonymity could not be guaranteed. Guessing can be accurate.

Cost–benefit analysis in qualitative research

So far this chapter has laid out the relationship between the intention and procedures of qualitative work and the way in which this can generate ethical dilemmas for researchers in forensic settings. It has been suggested that in general useful guiding principles for such research include consideration of the impact of the setting of research on the information available and received, to respect the confidentiality of information and to provide anonymity where possible to research participants.

A difficult question to answer is whether it is ever reasonable to compromise these goals in pursuit of the benefits to be had through the publication of the research; in this context improvements in service delivery would be an obvious 'good'. Roberts (1992, p.188) argues that the objective of the research may not coincide with the needs or desires of the respondents, but it may lead indirectly to improvements that are felt by participants to be necessary and therefore benefit other people. That the research could have a positive effect on others in the future is often a feature of the motivation to participate in research (Roberts 1992, p.183). Whether the relationship between publication and improvements is immediate or direct enough for participants to forgo their privacy could be merely a convenient assumption on the part of researchers.

Given the potential meaningfulness and thus accessibility of qualitative research findings for research participants, research publication could have immediate effects on participants (see, for example, Parry-Cooke 2000). Another potentially naïve assumption by researchers is the consciousness-raising potential of research or providing 'explanations of women's [or men's] lives that are useful to them as an instrument to improve their situations' (Edwards 1993, pp.183–184). Whilst this idea is rooted in researchers' duty to minimise the risk (indeed, likelihood) of affecting the research participant/setting, there is a danger that wishful researchers will transform this risk into a benefit for participants, under the guise of empowerment. Kelly, Burton and Regan (1994, p.37) offer a reality check, suggesting that on the whole participation in research will not radically alter people's lives. What remains is the risk of causing changes in attitudes, personality or self-concept, for good or ill. Participants may come to recognise, confront and question issues to which they previously had not given any consideration – for example, the realisation of fears and concerns. This is more likely in qualitative research where participants are encouraged to explore and articulate feelings and perceptions in ways and depths that they may not have done previously. This is avoided to some extent in quantitative research where the research instruments and findings appear to rely on wilfully obscure and inherently elitist discipline-specific academic constructs – though this creates ethical problems of its own.

CONCLUSION

The issues discussed in this chapter have wider consequences for research generally. The inaccurate presentation of findings through dilution and editing is damaging to the ethos and purpose of qualitative research. The constraints of forensic settings explored in this chapter may hinder research into the kind of sensitive and/or highly political issues that qualitative research usually examines. Research is regarded to be sensitive if there are potential consequences or implications for the participants in the research or for the class of individuals represented by the research (Sieber and Stanley 1988). Research is 'threatening' if it could cause participants to feel guilt, shame or embarrassment (Renzetti and Lee 1993, p.4), as in studies examining personal experiences, deviance and social control (Renzetti and Lee 1993, p.6) – those very issues which are within the remit of qualitative researchers in forensic settings.

It would be regrettable if original and useful research were not carried out as a result of researchers being deterred by the perception of such research as threatening or sensitive. Conducting research in atypical circumstances with complex settings, issues or people is a challenge to which researchers must respond. New, more flexible ways of obtaining full, voluntary, informed consent and collecting data must be created and developed to gain access to and give a voice to groups who might ordinarily be ignored on the grounds of being 'too difficult' or 'incoherent'. In order to be able to continue to pursue high-profile, sensitive research, new methods must be developed for protecting the identities of participants and their families whilst fully exploiting the available data. The involvement of consumers in research may provide insight into how this could be achieved. To give more power to those who are normally the subjects of research should not only provide a new perspective on how to conceal and protect participant's identities, but also challenge the kinds of data and the motivation for conducting research that researchers currently have. It must be asked whether current research is gaining access to people whose voices are underrepresented, and whether dominant research paradigms allow them to speak. This is an overriding ethical issue that emerges from consideration of qualitative research but perhaps has equally great implications, if not more, for quantitative research.

REFERENCES

Ashworth Inquiry (1992) Blom-Cooper, L. *et al.* (1992). Report of the Committee of Inquiry into Complaints about Ashworth Hospital. London: HMSO.

Ashworth Inquiry (1999) Fallon, P., Bluglass, R., Edwards, B. and Daniels, E. (1999) Report of the Committee of Inquiry into the Personality Disorder Unit, Ashworth Special Hospital. London: The Stationery Office.

Cardoza-Freeman, I. (1984) *The Joint: Language and Culture in a Maximum Security Prison.* Springfield USA: Charles C. Thomas.

Carpenter, W., Gold, J., Lahti, A., Queern, C., Conley, R., Bartko, J., Kovnick, J. and Appelbaum, P. (2000) 'Decisional Capacity for Informed Consent in Schizophrenia Research.' *Archives of General Psychiatry 57*, 6, 533–538.

Davidson, R.T. (1974) *Chicano Prisoners: The Key to San Quentin.* Prospect Heights, Illinois: Waveland Press.

Edwards, R. (1993) 'An Education in Interviewing: Placing the Researcher and the Research.' In C. Renzetti and R. Lee (eds) *Researching Sensitive Topics.* London: Sage.

GMC (undated) *Confidentiality: Protecting and Providing Information.* London: GMC.

Hassell, Y. and Bartlett, A. (2001) 'The Changing Climate for Women Patients in Medium Secure Units.' *Psychiatric Bulletin 25*, 340–342.

Heidensohn, F. (1985) *Women and Crime.* Basingstoke: MacMillan.

Hofman, M., Mueller-Spahn, F., Malhi, G. and Farmer, A. (1999) 'Consent and Ethics.' *International Journal of Psychiatry in Clinical Practice 3*, 4, 297–298.

Kelly, L. Burton, S. and Regan, L. (1994) 'Researching Women's Lives or Studying Women's Oppression? Reflections on What Constitutes Feminist Research.' In M. Maynard and J. Purvis (eds) *Researching Women's Lives from a Feminist Perspective.* London: Taylor & Francis.

Law Society and British Medical Association (1995) *The Assessment of Mental Capacity: Guidance for Doctors and Lawyers.* London: BMA.

Parry-Cooke, G. (2000) *Good Girls: Surviving the Secure System. A Consultation with Women in High and Medium Secure Settings.* London: University of North London.

Peay, J. (1989) *Tribunals on Trial: Study on Decision Making in the Mental Health Act 1983.* Oxford: Oxford University Press.

Pinals, D., Malhotra, A., Breier, A. and Pickar, D. (1998) 'Informed Consent in Schizophrenia Research.' *Psychiatric Services 49*, 2, 244.

Renzetti, C. and Lee, R. (eds) (1993) *Researching Sensitive Topics.* Sage: London.

Roberts, H. (1992) 'Answering Back: The Role of Respondents in Women's Health Research.' In H. Roberts (ed) *Women's Health Matters.* London: Routledge.

Rogers, A., Pilgrim, D. and Lacey, R. (1993) *Experiencing Psychiatry: Users' Views of Services.* Basingstoke: MacMillan.

Sieber & Stanley (1988)

Sieber, J. and Stanley, B. (1988) 'Ethical and Professional Dimensions of Socially Sensitive Research.' *American Psychologist, 42*, 49–55.

CASES

Re C (Adult: Refusal of treatment) [1994] 1 Weekly Law Reports 290.

ENDNOTES

1. Although the individual case study is a qualitative approach, this will not be considered in this chapter as it is well known within medical circles, frequently used and subject to clear guidance from the General Medical Council (GMC).

2. Each of the authors conducted one of the projects and both were involved in the third.

3. We are not concerned here with the bureaucratic issues of access through either host institutions or their ethics committees. Both have relatively little experience of assessing qualitative projects and can be ill prepared to review them; this is apparent from the application form for the South London Multi-centre Research Ethics Committee (MREC), which is clearly designed with quantitative projects in mind.

4. This seems in practice, even where explicit consent is given, now to have extended to blanket anonymity for research participants, possibly losing sight of the fundamental purpose of confidentiality.

CHAPTER 5

Ethical Issues in Risk Assessment Practice and Research

Caroline Logan

INTRODUCTION

Risk assessment is an estimation of the likelihood of the occurrence of a hazardous event based on our awareness of the importance and presence of certain conditions that we assume to be risk factors; traditionally, risk assessment is a prediction. Risk assessments in relation to violent behaviour are often undertaken in forensic and other clinical settings (e.g. Babiker and Arnold 1997; Grubin 1999; Motz 2001; Shea 1997; Quinsey *et al.* 1998). Important ethical issues are raised as a result of both the clinical management of violence risk and research into this subject, and these are the subject of this chapter.

The chapter begins with a brief review of current practice in violence risk assessment. A range of ethical issues arising from the current practice of such assessments, in clinical and forensic settings in particular, will then be discussed. Specifically, ethical issues bridging the clinical and research domains – such as duty to inform, choice of risk assessment procedure, communicating findings, and whether there exists an acceptable level of risk – will be considered. The chapter concludes with recommendations for ways in which violence risk can be assessed and managed whilst retaining an optimal level of ethical responsibility, both to the public and to the client.

REVIEW OF RISK ASSESSMENT PRACTICE

There are two broad approaches to the assessment of risk: actuarial and clinical. The different approaches are frequently compared (e.g. Gardner *et al.* 1996; Grove *et al.* 2000; Mossman 1994) and it is clear that some work remains to be done to establish the optimal use for examples of each approach. I discuss each approach in more detail below.

Actuarial risk assessment

Actuarial risk assessment derives a quantitative estimate of the likelihood that an individual will act violently during a given time period, based on an evaluation of those characteristics that have been shown to statistically differentiate those who are violent subsequently from those who are not. These characteristics, known as risk factors, are often assigned different weights reflecting their importance in the final predictive equation. The number of risk factors present in any individual, in combination with their weight, is associated with a likelihood of reoffending. This likelihood can be expressed as a percentage or a risk classification (low, medium, high), which represents the known reoffending rate among individuals in the original research. An assumption is made, therefore, that if the individual being assessed shares the same risk factors as a research sample with a known reoffence rate, then that individual has a likelihood of reoffending comparable to that observed in the sample.

Thus, actuarial risk assessment is similar to buying car insurance. A customer provides a company with information about 'risk factors' (e.g. gender, age, postcode, type of car, number of previous accidents, and so on). The company enters this information into its database and compares the customer with similar other customers about whom information on number of claims is already known. A 'risk assessment' is made, and the driver is allocated to the appropriate insurance band with related charges, so that high-risk drivers pay more based on the estimated probability of making a claim in the year ahead.

Probably the best-known protocol for the actuarial assessment of violence risk is the Violence Risk Appraisal Guide (VRAG – Quinsey *et al.* 1998; Webster *et al.* 1994). This 12-item protocol was developed from a retrospective study carried out at Oak Ridge Hospital, which is a maximum security forensic psychiatric facility in Ontario in Canada. The VRAG has good predictive validity (Rice and Harris 1995, 1997), but more recent forms of actuarial risk assessment, such as the iterative classification tree method developed by the MacArthur risk assessment study, have produced results suggestive of better predictive validity than has been achieved by the VRAG (Monahan *et al.* 2001).

Actuarial risk assessment methods promote good predictive accuracy. Such methods generate confidence that discrimination – those who will and will not reoffend – will be good, and that the right people – those who will reoffend – will be identified and, as a result, effectively managed to reduce their risk of violence or sexual violence. However, there are three limitations to the use of actuarial methods. First, the items that make up actuarial instruments have been derived solely from empirical research. Characteristics that are difficult to research (e.g. violent fantasies) or occur infrequently (e.g. threats to kill or injure) are unlikely to be included in an actuarial risk assessment instrument despite their clinical relevance. Second, actuarial methods are comprised almost entirely of static factors that are unlikely to change (e.g. separated from parents before age 16 years). Even if they do change (e.g. marital status), the relationship between the changed static factor and future risk may not be very rational. Also not very rational is the fact that successful completion of a violence reduction programme, effective post-release supervision, even severe disability, would not make a difference to the outcome of an actuarial risk prediction. Finally, actuarial risk assessment is the outcome of a descriptive review of factors statistically correlated with violence and does not represent any theory about the aetiology of such behaviour. Consequently, the emphasis is on the detection of mainly clinically obsolete risk factors and not on the detection of violence risk factors open to change.

Structured clinical judgement approaches to risk assessment

Clinical assessments of risk may be structured or unstructured. Unstructured clinical judgement has been criticised for lacking reliability and validity (Grove and Meehl 1996). However, using a systematic assessment procedure, it is possible to structure clinical judgements of risk in ways that maintain a clinical focus whilst maximising reliability and validity.

Approaches utilising structured clinical judgement – sometimes referred to as structured professional guidelines – advocate the measurement of variables that are both static and dynamic, and encourage the monitoring of risk factors in order to detect changes in risk over time and in response to preventative or risk management procedures or relevant other changed circumstances (e.g. disability). Thus, the emphasis of such approaches is on prevention rather than prediction, and the underlying assumption is that overall risk is dynamic rather than stable. However, although more rational than are empirically based actuarial approaches, the theoretical basis of structured clinical judgement approaches is similarly weak.

The most popular example of violence risk assessment by structured clinical judgement is the HCR-20 (Webster *et al.* 1997). The HCR-20 is a set of guidelines for use by clinicians in their assessment of historical, clinical and risk management factors relevant to violent behaviour in male or female offenders or patients with a history of mental health needs (e.g. mental disorder, personality disorder). Guidelines were developed from reviews of the scientific, professional and legal literatures and reflect common-sense clinical practice as well as empirical research.

Structured clinical judgement approaches appeal to clinicians as they support and endeavour to improve upon what clinicians already do rather than propose that clinical judgement is flawed and in need of supplement, if not replacement, by actuarial methods (as proposed by Quinsey *et al.* 1998).

However, structured clinical judgement methods also have their limitations. While such methods direct clinicians on the risk factors to assess and how to assess them, the final formulation is the responsibility of the clinician and the product of induction, and therefore still subject to problems with reliability and possibly validity also. Yet actuarial risk assessment is subject to the same limitation: researchers prescribe how practitioners should conduct risk assessments, but not how they should incorporate the findings into their formulation or risk management plan.

In summary, there are two main methods of conducting risk assessments: clinical judgement (structured and unstructured) and actuarial risk assessment. Unstructured clinical judgement, whilst common, is significantly affected by problems with reliability and validity and is greatly improved by any method that structures the risk assessment process. Structured clinical judgement methods, such as the HCR-20, set good practice parameters that systematise and make explicit clinical assessment with the aid of known risk factors. Actuarial risk assessment (e.g. the VRAG) is a tightly prescribed form of evaluation intended to override unstructured clinical judgement if not replace with a quantified measure of risk. The two approaches each have their strengths and limitations in terms of dependence on an empirical and theoretical base, attention to common-sense clinical practice, and respect for both reliability and validity. However, their advantages and disadvantages may also be considered in terms of their ethical implications in research and practice, and it is to these that we will now turn.

ETHICAL ISSUES IN RISK ASSESSMENT PRACTICE AND RESEARCH

Ethical first principles

In any clinical or health care context, ethics are the rules of competent, responsible, accountable and respectful engagement. The ethical guidelines endorsed by professional bodies are general standards to which all clinical practice should aspire, and cover such issues as competency, integrity, social and scientific responsibility, and respect for the rights, dignity and welfare of others. Four specific moral principles have been described as applying to health care practice and research (Blackburn 2002; Bloch, Chodoff and Green 1999; Kitchener 1984). These four principles provide a useful framework for the consideration of a number of general ethical issues in violence risk assessment.

Respect for autonomy refers to respect for the decision making capacities of autonomous individuals who are free to choose their own courses of action provided that this does not violate the autonomy of others. Where capacity for free choice is impaired or restricted, those providing care are in a position to overrule what the client wants in direct challenge to the principle of autonomy. Such a situation can lead to the subtle problem of how to care for clients respectfully and without rendering them fearful or threatened (Beauchamp 1999). Many dilemmas in health care involve questions about the conditions under which a client's right to autonomous expression demands action by others and how such situations can or should be managed to avoid paternalism and even abuse.

Beneficence requires that practitioners help others to further their important and legitimate interests, often by preventing or removing possible harms (Beauchamp 1999). In medicine, good is done by the alleviation of disease or disability and the reduction of pain and suffering. Beneficence is often balanced against *non-maleficence*: the principle of doing no harm. In general, however, potential harms are balanced against the predicted benefits; for example, psychotropic medication reduces distress-ing psychotic symptoms but can have unpleasant side-effects. In forensic mental health, social good can be done by managing the liberty of individ-ual clients, which results in the control of violence risk.

Finally, the ethical principle of *justice* refers to fairness in the distribution of benefits and risks or the principle of equal persons being treated equally. However, different theories of justice exist. Egalitarian theories emphasise equal access to primary goods and services; libertarian theories emphasise rights to social and economic liberty; and utilitarian theories emphasise a mixed use of such criteria so that public and private utility are maximised (Beauchamp 1999). The general principle of justice is captured by all three theories but a different use of the principle is emphasised in each.

The following section describes a number of issues in risk assessment practice and research that raise concerns of an ethical nature relevant to each of the principles described above and indicate the need for the greater speci-fication of ethical guidelines in this area of assessment.

Ethical issues in risk assessment practice

Respect for autonomy: who is the client in risk assessment?

The client of a psychological assessment is traditionally the person on whom the assessment is performed. The purpose of such an assessment is usually the determination of some aspect of the mental state of the individ-ual in order that the appropriate intervention can be identified and carried out, resulting in positive change and the relief of distressing symptoms. Such a cause and effect model is not clearly the case in assessments of risk.

In risk assessment, a client is assessed more often than not because such an evaluation is required by others in order to serve their wish for protection from the client. The client may co-operate with the risk assessment, although actuarial forms of risk assessment do not require the co-operation or even the knowledge of the client that such an assessment is being carried out. However, he or she has little or no say in the outcome of the assessment or in the dissemination of its findings; the client is given little opportunity to exercise autonomy. Further, practitioners may morally justify their decision to deny or restrict the autonomy of their clients because, by their past or future threatened behaviour, clients have demonstrated a willingness to place their needs ahead of those of others, potentially to their detriment; in effect clients don't deserve to have their rights respected when they have abused the rights of others. Practitioners therefore could be seen to be acting more in service of the institutions who employ them than the clients in their care by their willingness to deny their clients autonomy.

Actuarial risk assessment makes clear challenges to the notion that the client is the one being served in assessments of risk. Whilst their use by some professional groups (e.g. police, probation) is practically and even ethically viable – for instance, to determine the supervision and monitoring require- ments of individuals about to be released from detention and the more general distribution of limited resources – their use by clinical professionals (e.g. clinical psychologists, psychiatrists) is of more concern. Actuarial methods need not require any contact with the client, and they provide cli- nicians with little or no guidance on the interpretation of findings and their incorporation into competent, responsible, accountable and respectful risk management plans. For example, the determination of a 44 per cent proba- bility of violent reoffence in the seven years following assessment translates into no clear strategy for violence reduction and prevention because such an assessment is a statement about the client's membership of a group with a corresponding likelihood of violent behaviour, rather than a determination of case-specific risk factors or potential.

Thus, it is clearly the needs of others that are served by such a method that seeks to identify risky individuals rather than deal with them, and it is the practice of the clinical professions that is most challenged by their use. Structured clinical judgement approaches, on the other hand, encourage if not necessitate client participation and emphasise the identification of con- ditions in which that person's risk to others would become unacceptable. Therefore, the means of identifying the strategies that would manage the risks identified using structured clinical approaches provide for a more accountable system in which the needs of the client are more evenly balanced against those of the general public and specific third parties.

Beneficence and non-maleficence in risk assessment: whose information is it?
According to the principle of beneficence, clinicians have an ethical respon- sibility to do good to their clients and to eliminate unnecessary suffering. Arguably, the way in which the results of risk assessments are communicated to others is an area in which beneficence may be served – or breached. Risk assessment generates information that can powerfully affect the lives not

only of the person being assessed, but others known or even unknown. Both clinicians and researchers face profound ethical dilemmas about the use of this information.

Clinicians may be influenced by the case of *Tarasoff* v. *Regents of the University of California*, which defined (in the USA at least) the extent of the clinician's duties to disclose information about risk to others. Tatiana Tarasoff was murdered by a man who had revealed to his therapist his intention to harm her. The therapist was held legally liable because, although he informed the university security department and others of his concerns about his client, he failed to inform Ms Tarasoff herself (*Tarasoff* v. *Regents of the University of California* 1974, 1976). As a consequence of this case, it is now accepted that where a client provides information that leads the therapist to conclude that there is a more than likely risk of harm to an identifiable third party, there is an ethical and legal duty to warn or protect the potential victim despite the almost sacrosanct duty of confidentiality that exists in the usual therapist–client interactions.

In violence risk assessment, where potential to harm others is directly assessed, duty to inform is a frequently encountered obligation. This duty applies not only to clinicians regarding their clients and third parties but also to researchers (Monahan *et al.* 1993). Ways have to be found to achieve a balance between the benefits of risk disclosure, which might result in the prevention of possible harm, and the potentially negative effect, on both therapeutic and research relationships with clients, that disclosure would have.

Structured clinical judgement methods, which combine interview data with collateral information, create more opportunities to determine the existence of potential victims and to manage risk factors than actuarial methods. Clinical risk assessment methods, which emphasise prevention rather than simple prediction, contain the means by which identified risks may be managed *and* made obvious to the client. Thus, structured clinical more than actuarial methods counter potential maleficence – prediction without responsibility for change – with the means by which beneficent practice may be undertaken, rendering possible something approximating a balance between good to the client *and* the protection of potential victims.

If clinicians are to demonstrate good to their clients as well as to the general public, a more just form of communication is one in which clients, and those who are charged with supervising them, are given advice about ways by which they can reduce or manage the risks they pose to others using achievable means. Accountability and transparency in risk decision making, as well as communication about adjustable rather than static risk, are more likely to enhance client co-operation and collaboration with risk management (Heilbrun 1997). Again, some forms of risk assessment support the transparent and beneficent communication of findings, and so the choice of risk assessment method is as much an ethical one as it is practical.

Respect for justice: 1. Bias and prejudice

Issues about disclosure and communication raise concerns not only about beneficence but also about the fair and equitable treatment of individuals whose risks are being assessed. However, it is of concern that many risk assessment measures have been derived from only a narrow range of offenders, and cannot be applied to other offenders in other locations without the introduction of bias and prejudice. The VRAG is a good example. Developed in North America, it is intended only for use with male, mentally disordered offenders in high secure forensic psychiatric care. The use of the VRAG in any other setting is undertaken without it being clear that it works in the same way as it did in the original sample.

The VRAG fails to serve the fair and equitable treatment of offenders in other ways. For example, the VRAG was developed from a retrospective research study (Webster *et al.* 1994); the 12 component items were selected on the basis of their ability to 'postdict' violent recidivism over seven- and ten-year periods. Evidence of the *pre*dictive validity of the VRAG only became available from 2001 (Harris *et al.* 2002), bringing into question the confidence with which this measure can be used as a predictive instrument in any locality. Further, the specification of lengthy periods of time over which level of assessed risk is expected to be stable and unaltered by any treatment or management programme creates assessments of risk that cannot change regardless of the efforts of the client or those managing him – so-called 'black hole' risk assessments – and is contrary to the common-sense view that risk is context-specific.

Consequently, an individual may find him or herself assessed as high risk for an indefinite period based on instruments that cannot be said for certain to be reliable or valid. Given that deprivation of liberty is a potential consequence of such a finding, there is an onus on both clinicians and researchers to develop, select and apply measures in a just way. This point is particularly applicable to clients from ethnic minorities who are over-represented in forensic settings. How can the ethical claims of clients be served – and balanced against those of the general public – by the use of instruments whose cross-cultural reliability and predictive validity have not yet been established, whose use is one-off and condemnatory, and without the capacity to monitor and respond to change evident in practice in mental health care in other contexts?

Respect for justice: 2. What is an acceptable level of risk?
Actuarial methods of risk assessment quantify risk for future violence or sexual violence, usually as a probability estimate. By quantifying risk, the question of what is an acceptable level of risk inevitably arises. Is an acceptable level of risk anything greater than 50 per cent (i.e. violence is more likely than not to occur), around 20 per cent, or zero per cent? Can anyone, especially someone with a history of violence, ever be considered to be no risk at all? If an acceptable level of risk is not or is unlikely to be zero, how much risk is acceptable? Also, is a low risk of committing an act of serious violence such as murder better than a high risk of minor assault? Ethically, how can any level of known and measured risk be acceptable – and who should take the decision?

Ethical issues in risk assessment research

Duty to inform in the context of risk assessment research presents a different set of demands from those encountered in clinical practice; to what extent are researchers responsible for preventing the occurrence of violent behaviour in research participants (Appelbaum and Rosenbaum 1989)? Where participants are interviewed for data collection purposes, the opportunity exists for them to divulge information about potential victims or make threats to the safety of the researchers themselves. If researchers are presented with such information and they respond to their duty to inform, they effectively compromise their observations by determining the dependent variable – in this case, absence of violence. Can the data from such participants be legitimately included in studies in which risk assessment is the objective? The answer to such a question has to be no as the data derived are not the result of impartial observation. However, the fault in this case would appear to lie with the design of research studies in which response to the duty to inform is either discouraged or penalised.

Research methods need to be developed that will allow researchers to respond to their duty to inform without being penalised through data loss or feeling compromised for so doing. Clinicians (arguably) have a moral responsibility to prevent violence and sexual violence in those whom they suspect the potential for such behaviour. The moral responsibilities of researchers in the field of risk assessment are more remote from those of the clinician and actuarial methods of risk assessment generally support such distance, by their emphasis on historical or static factors and because interviewing participants is generally not necessary. Research using actuarial risk assessment instruments is therefore easy to undertake compared with research utilising structured clinical judgement approaches, where issues of training, inter-rater reliability and client co-operation tend to limit the numbers of participants and extend the length of time required to complete data collection.

However, as has been suggested above, actuarial risk assessment is less supportive of the highest standards of ethical clinical practice in violence management than are structured clinical methods. Is this a case of good scientific research failing to support or being in competition with the demand for good and ethical clinical practice when surely the object of science is to provide the means by which practitioners can improve upon the benefits they are trained to impart to their clients? The legal obligation on those who work with violent and sexually violent offenders to predict those who will reoffend appears to have superseded the clinical standards practitioners are ethically obliged to advocate. And researchers in the field of prediction have failed to grasp the necessity of developing methodologies that measure risk management success, preferring instead the convenience of mere summation.

SUMMARY AND RECOMMENDATIONS

Four basic ethical principles provide a starting point for moral judgements in health care. They are – or should be – as applicable in the domain of violence and sexual violence risk assessment as they are elsewhere in health and mental health care practice. However, a review of some of the ethical challenges posed by risk assessment makes clear that these principles do not treat nor offer any guidance on the resolution of the subtleties of those challenges. Consequently, it is possible if not highly likely that current risk assessment practice could be in direct contravention of recommended standards if not, on some occasions and using some methods, clearly unethical. Actuarial risk assessment would appear to be the most guilty party.

However, risk can be assessed reliably better than chance and (arguably) clinicians are ethically obliged to do something rather than nothing in response to repetitive or threatened violent behaviour. Ethically sensitive risk assessment practice, as undertaken by clinicians, should contain the following characteristics as a minimum requirement. First, risk assessment undertaken by the clinical professions should be closely allied to risk management; what is assessed should be what is capable of change with a commensurate effect on the risks assessed. Although they have predictive validity and their measurement in actuarial scales is useful in some contexts, static factors are difficult if not impossible to incorporate into risk management and change in risk cannot be reasonably determined by any remeasurement of marital status or age at index offence. Clients should not be put in the position of being rated as high risk without the capacity to demonstrate change over time or in response to treatment or careful management.

Second, practitioners should utilise methods of risk assessment that promote transparency in decision making in order to improve their accountability to the clients and the general public that they serve. By maximising accountability to clients, there is a greater than otherwise chance of keeping clients engaged in interventions and risk management arrangements. Structured clinical judgement methods of risk assessment would appear to promote the most ethical practice in this kind of assessment. Actuarial risk assessment methods would appear, by this evaluation, to promote the least ethical practice. Ethical practice must supersede psychometric purism.

Although professional guidelines about ethical practice in clinical settings exist, and practitioners should be familiar with them, they are insufficiently worked out to meet the ethical demands being made in relation to risk assessment of violence. Current guidelines are very supportive of the principle of ethical practice but are not specific about the means by which such practice can be achieved such as to limit the likelihood that litigation will dictate the ethical practices of psychologists in the years to come

(Logan, Dolan and Doyle 2001; Monahan *et al.* 1993). Therefore, professional bodies may need to be more prescriptive in anticipation of the litigation their members could otherwise face.

Lastly, research should facilitate ethical risk assessment practice by attempting to measure the means by which changes in risk can be demonstrated and followed up over time and violence prevented rather than observed (Douglas and Kropp 2002). Practitioners should no longer be constrained by researchers who are unable to measure the variables that promote their best – and ethical – practice.

REFERENCES

Appelbaum, P. and Rosenbaum, A. (1989) 'Tarasoff and the Researcher: Does the Duty to Protect Apply in the Research Setting?' *American Psychologist* 44, 885–894.

Babiker, G. and Arnold, L. (1997) *The Language of Injury: Comprehending Self-mutilation.* Leicester: The British Psychological Society.

Beauchamp, T. (1999) 'The Philosophical Basis of Psychiatric Ethics.' In S. Bloch, P. Chodoff and S. Green (eds) *Psychiatric Ethics* (3rd edition). New York: Oxford University Press, 25–48.

Blackburn, R. (2002) 'Ethical Issues in Motivating Offenders to Change.' In M. McMurran (ed) *Motivating Offenders to Change: A Guide to Enhancing Engagement in Therapy.* Chichester: Wiley.

Bloch, S., Chodoff, P. and Green, S. (1999) *Psychiatric Ethics* (3rd edition). New York: Oxford University Press.

Douglas, K. and Kropp, P. (2002) 'A Prevention-based Paradigm for Violence Risk Assessment: Clinical and Research Applications.' *Criminal Justice and Behaviour 29*, 617–658.

Gardner, W., Lidz, C., Mulvey, E. and Shaw, E. (1996) 'Clinical versus Actuarial Predictions of Violence in Patients with Mental Illnesses.' *Journal of Consulting and Clinical Psychology 64*, 602–609.

Grove, W. and Meehl, P. (1996) 'Comparative Efficiency of Informal (Subjective, Impressionistic) and Formal (Mechanical, Algorithmic) Prediction Procedures: The Clinical-statistical Controversy.' *Psychology, Public Policy, and Law 2*, 293–323.

Grove, W., Zald, D., Lebow, B., Snitz, B. and Nelson, C. (2000) 'Clinical versus Mechanical Prediction: A Meta-analysis.' *Psychological Assessment 12,* 19–30.

Harris, G.T., Rice, M.E. and Cormier, C.A. (2002) 'Prospective Replication of the Violence Risk Appraisal Guide in Predicting Violent Recidivism among Forensic Patients.' *Law and Human Behaviour 26,* 4, 377–394.

Grubin, D. (1999) 'Actuarial and Clinical Assessment of Risk in Sex Offenders.' *Journal of Interpersonal Violence 14,* 331–343.

Heilbrun, K. (1997) 'Prediction versus Management Models Relevant to Risk Assessment: The Importance of Legal Decision-making Context.' *Law and Human Behaviour 21,* 347–359.

Kitchener, K. (1984) 'Intuition, Critical Evaluation and Ethical Principles: The Foundation for Ethical Decisions in Counseling Psychology.' *The Counseling Psychologist 12,* 43–56.

Logan, C., Dolan, M. and Doyle, M. (2001) *Ethics in Risk Assessment: Actuarial and Structured Professional Guidelines Methods Compared.* Paper presented at the International Conference on Violence Risk Assessment and Management, Sundsvall, Sweden, November.

Monahan, J., Appelbaum, P., Mulvey, E., Robbins, P. and Lidz, C. (1993) 'Ethical and Legal Duties in Conducting Research on Violence: Lessons from the MacArthur Risk Assessment Study.' *Violence and Victims 8,* 387–396.

Monahan, J., Steadman, H., Silver, E., Appelbaum, P., Robbins, P., Mulvey, E., Roth, L., Grisso, T. and Banks, S. (2001) *Rethinking Risk Assessment: The MacArthur Study of Mental Disorder and Violence.* New York: Oxford University Press.

Mossman, D. (1994) 'Assessing Predictions of Violence: Being Accurate about Accuracy.' *Journal of Consulting and Clinical Psychology 62,* 783–792.

Motz, A. (2001) *The Psychology of Female Violence: Crimes against the Body.* Hove: Brunner-Routledge.

Quinsey, V., Harris, G., Rice, M. and Cormier, C. (1998) *Violent Offenders: Appraising and Managing Risk.* Washington DC: American Psychological Association.

Rice, M. and Harris, G. (1995) 'Violent Recidivism: Assessing Predictive Validity.' *Journal of Consulting and Clinical Psychology 63,* 737–748.

Rice, M. and Harris, G. (1997) 'Cross Validation and Extension of the Violence Risk Appraisal Guide for Child Molesters and Rapists.' *Law and Human Behaviour 21,* 231–241.

Shea, S. (1997) *The Practical Art of Suicide Assessment.* New York: John Wiley & Sons Inc.

Webster, C., Harris, G., Rice, M., Cormier, C. and Quinsey, V. (1994) *The Violence Prediction Scheme: Assessing Dangerousness in High Risk Men.* Toronto, Canada: Centre of Criminology, University of Toronto.

Webster, C., Douglas, K., Eaves, D. and Hart, S. (1997) *HCR-20: Assessing Risk for Violence* (2nd edition). Vancouver: Mental Health, Law and Policy Institute, Simon Fraser University and the British Columbia Forensic Psychiatric Services Commission.

CASES

Tarasoff v. *Regents of the University of California* [1974] 118 Cal Rptr, 129, 529 P.2d 553.

Tarasoff v. *Regents of the University of California* [1976] 17 Cal 3d 425, 551 P. 2d 334.

CHAPTER 6

Multi-disciplinary Aspects of Forensic Mental Health Research

Tom Mason

INTRODUCTION

Mankind has by nature a herding instinct that would appear to serve the functions of survival, protection and procreation. However, herding alone is an insufficient explanation to account for the success of the human race in the overall scheme of the world's development. Those animals that not only have the capacity to group together but also to work together to achieve a common objective appear to be more successful than those who operate alone. Furthermore, working as a group in which there are a number of roles to fulfil to achieve a common objective would indicate that the more effective each member becomes, the more effective the group becomes. The corollary of this suggests that the roles become increasingly complex and specialised and that each member formulates distinct areas of expertise.

In contemporary society, working within a team approach to achieve a common aim is regarded as the most effective strategy for many complex tasks, from sports to science and from business to engineering. Again, this is based on a reductionist approach in which functional roles are increasingly specialised and areas of expertise are brought together to contribute to the overall objective. However, in contemporary teams from many walks of life other factors are brought into play and do affect the operation of the group approach. These factors include the human vagaries of ambition, power, status, relationships and so on. Hence, some teams are more successful, in terms of achieving their overall objective, than others.

Working within a multi-disciplinary team in forensic mental health practice shares the same dynamic outlined above but is also highly complex for a number of reasons. First, the professional area of practice is developing rather than established. Second, it draws on a multi-professional group (psychiatry, psychology, nursing etc.) who are seeking to adapt their general psychiatric knowledge base to a population of mentally disordered offenders. Third, the objectives of the profession are not fully agreed upon and therefore the outcomes are ill defined. Finally, the patient group is, by and large, compulsorily detained against their wishes and forced to have treatment that they otherwise may not want.

This chapter will deal first with the dynamics of the multi-disciplinary team in forensic practice and highlight the issues of researching sensitive topics. Second, the main ethical concerns of working within, and facing, multi-disciplinary teams will be outlined. Finally, research obstacles and strategies for overcoming them will be highlighted from research practice examples.

MULTI-DISCIPLINARY WORKING

The literature on multi-disciplinary team working would suggest that it is both a confused and confusing concept which is dependent, for definitional purposes, on personal interpretations and differing contexts (Cott 1998; Moss 1994). For example, Drinka and Ray (1987) employed a positive approach in claiming that teamwork comprised of 'multiple health disciplines with diverse knowledge and skills who share an integrated set of goals and who utilise interdependent collaboration that makes communication, sharing of knowledge, and co-ordination of services to provide services to patients and their care giving systems'. On the other hand, the National Health Service Executive (1993) adopted a negative framework by focusing upon what factors contributed to failed teamwork: 'Rigid role demarcation, tradition, vested professional interests, poor communication leading to confusion and misunderstanding about responsibilities have all been blamed for lack of progress'. However, despite this lack of clarity regarding multi-disciplinary team working, it continues to be considered as a desirable and necessary endeavour for those concerned in the enterprise (McGrath 1993; Roberts and Priest 1997).

Focusing specifically on the forensic domain, the literature on multi-disciplinary team working is conspicuous by its absence. However, two pieces of work can be cited as starting points. First, Williams, Vivian-Byrne and Mason (2000) undertook a research project on team working in a medium secure unit and found that whilst individual members of a team operated within codes of practice there was little cross-referencing of these codes across professional groups. They also reported that individual members adopted an ethical code of referral at three levels: (a) within their own individual ideologies, (b) towards their organisation's philosophy or ethos, and (c) in relation to their profession's code of conduct. The tensions and conflicts within this ethical referral system produced a complex dynamic that made operational practice difficult for patients to pre-judge. Second, Brooker and Whyte (2000) conducted research into multi-disciplinary team working in secure psychiatric environments which ranged from prison settings through to low secure units. The key findings, relevant to this chapter, were: (a) effective multi-disciplinary team working required senior personnel and middle managers to provide organisational legitimacy and exert significant influence; (b) professional disciplines required specialist training in order to function as a team; and (c) effective team working depends as much on interpersonal skills as on inter-professional collaboration.

RESEARCHING SENSITIVE ISSUES

At one level in both scientific and lay populations the notion of undertaking research is, generally, considered a laudable and worthwhile enterprise, depending on the target of that investigation. Few commentators would argue that research into leukaemia, cystic fibrosis or diabetes is not welcomed, yet the research into stem cells, cloning and artificial embryos makes many people uneasy. Similarly, research into the natural, or physical, world such as cosmology, vulcanology or meteorology receives a populist, if generally unconcerned, vote and yet social scientific research into racism, feminism or ageism jars with general sensitivities. Presumably, one reason for this relates to what the research actually reveals and its impact on the human race. Research that discovers a new atomic particle which may have a significant impact on our understanding of radiation cancer would be more welcomed than research that reveals systematic institutional prejudice in

British organisations. The argument proffered throughout this chapter is that there are various levels of human operations which have differing degrees of visibility, and research that reveals the hidden elements is generally unwelcome by those wishing to maintain their implicit nature.

Researching sensitive issues has received considerable attention by Lee (1993) and Renzetti and Lee (1993). These authors argued that a common problem in researching sensitive issues is that the term is used popularly as if it is self-explanatory. However, Sieber and Stanley (1988) made an early attempt to pin the concept down by defining it as 'studies in which there are potential consequences or implications, either directly for the participants in the research or for the class of individuals represented by the research'. Other authors have included specific contexts which make an issue sensitive to research (Brewer 1990) whilst others have argued it is the socio-political nature of the issue that gives it its sensitivity (Rostocki 1986). However, the generally agreed defining quality refers to research that causes some degree of threat, either to those under investigation or those undertaking the inquiry. Lee (1993) summed it up accordingly: 'sensitive topics present problems because research into them involves potential costs to those involved in the research, including, on occasion, the researcher'.

In discussing research as threat Lee (1993) highlighted three broad areas of threat: 1. intrusive threat, 2. threat of sanction, and 3. political threat. Intrusive threat is concerned with research that is conducted into the private domains of the individuals under study. These private areas may include such domains as someone's financial affairs or sexuality and are highly likely to be considered threatening. Threat of sanction involves research that may reveal something about the subjects under study which may be used against them at a later stage. This has been termed 'the fear of scrutiny' by Payne *et al.* (1980) and has contributed to many researchers in social science being considered a 'spy'. Political threat refers to the wider notion that all social science research must be considered as being located within a social, economic and political world. It is often considered as 'dangerous' as it may destabilise the status quo and challenge stakeholders' vested interests. It is particularly relevant to elite groups who have the power, resources and expertise to protect their interests and reputation.

In locating threats to the researcher Lee (1993) has defined four broad areas: 1. stigma contagion, 2. career dangers, 3. anonymous dangers, and 4. presentational dangers. Stigma contagion occurs when the researcher is stigmatised by the topic under investigation. For example, this has been noted when researchers studying male sexuality were considered to be homosexual, irrespective of whether or not they were (Lee 1993). Career dangers are said to occur when findings disrupt powerful stakeholders' interests and affect the researchers' jobs, promotions and professional development. Although higher managers may explicitly support research and make laudable commentary regarding the value of findings, implicitly they may be angry at the researcher for revealing what they consider to be negative results. Anonymous dangers concern threats to the researcher that arise from the situation under investigation. For example, research into policing in Northern Ireland or football hooliganism clearly places the researcher under threat. Finally, presentational dangers occur when the researcher, as a researcher, is revealed. This can occur in research into cults or illicit drug-trafficking.

Secure settings, psychiatric or otherwise, are notoriously difficult organisations to gain access to for research purposes and are predominantly considered 'closed institutions' (HMSO 1992; Mason 1997) – although, as we have seen above, explicitly many secure psychiatric hospitals and units make positive statements regarding research in their organisations but implicitly operate strategies of exclusion and obstruction. The reasons for this are complex but fit well with Lee's typology of intrusive threat, threat of sanction and political threat outlined above. This chapter will go some way in examining why multi-disciplinary groups in secure psychiatric settings may feel that research is threatening to them and will explicate some of the strategies of obstruction suggested above.

THE FRONTIERS OF THE FORENSIC ETHICAL ENTERPRISE

Ethics in health care is a complex affair. Most practitioners in health care settings fortunately ground their practice in the best interests of the patient with only a relative few intentionally setting out to do harm. When ethical standards are transgressed, there usually follows a public outcry, as in the cases of Beverly Allitt, a nurse who deliberately killed children whilst working on a hospital ward, Harold Shipman, a GP who systematically killed elderly people in his care, and the Alder Hey Children's Hospital organ donor scandal. Although rogue practitioners will always be a threat it is fair to say that the majority of individuals working in health care settings act within recognised moral boundaries. However, this is focusing upon the individual nature of human beings rather than on the social structures that they have formed, and it is this latter area of ethical analysis which requires careful scrutiny. The ethics involved in the social structures of generalised medicine do not appear too problematic as they have the single intention of acting in the patient's best interests. This carries with it the notion of *voluntariness* – that is, the patient wishes treatment and contributes willingly to the doctor–patient relationship (all other health care workers being subsumed within this relationship). Thus, the social system of physical health care involving hospitals, GP surgeries, emergency services, and so on, has evolved on the sound ethics rooted in the Hippocratic oath and refined through the Declaration of Geneva, Principles of Medical Ethics of the American Medical Association, and the Declaration of Helsinki, to name but a few ethical codes.

Turning to psychiatry we may well begin with similar statements as above – that is, the single intention of acting in the patient's best interests, grounded in the doctor–patient relationship. However, problems begin to emerge with the ethics of psychiatry (Bloch and Chodoff 1981). These problems involve questions relating to the extent to which the mental illness incapacitates the person from contributing to the doctor–patient relationship – even when the interface with psychiatry is voluntary. This is further complicated when this psychiatric interface is compulsorily enforced with the employment of the Mental Health Act (Berman and Segel 1982). Furthermore, if an element of the mental illness involves a threat towards others then the singleness of the doctor–patient relationship is modified by the need to consider others. However, the social structures involved in voluntary psychiatric practice, despite these emerging ethical difficulties, do appear to remain relatively intact, but only in so far as the patient is not coerced (Mason and Jennings 1997).

In forensic psychiatric practice, however, ethical problems loom large. Before dealing with these it seems important to make a distinction between the two types of 'forensic ethics' that are emerging in the literature. The first concerns forensic practitioners who evaluate 'subjects for the purpose of generating a report or test for an administrative or legal process' (Appelbaum 1997). This is usually a court report to establish the competency to stand trial. The second type of 'forensic ethics' relates to the functions of forensic practitioners in secure psychiatric settings and involves issues of clinical assessments and treatments. This involves all secure psychiatric services in hospitals, clinics and units who cater for mentally disordered offenders under mental health legislation – the two pivotal points being that they are (a) compulsorily detained against their wishes and (b) forced to have treatment that they may not wish to have. It is the latter area of 'forensic ethics' which is focused upon here.

COMPETING VALUE THEORIES IN THE MULTI-DISCIPLINARY TEAM

Forensic health care practitioners may be influenced to a greater or lesser degree by any one of the philosophical positions outlined below. In the working of the multi-disciplinary team, the web of competing value theories can become entangled.

1. Individualism

Individualism is concerned with personal freedom, independence and liberty from the effects of the attitudes and beliefs of others. At one level this has a positive connotation in that to choose one's own ideology whilst being free from others' dogma is clearly a personal freedom. However, at another level it can suggest a conflict between the accepted normative standards of a society or group and an individual's own behaviours which may be at odds with the wider group. A person who is deemed to be mentally disordered upholds his individual norms and beliefs in contradiction to the wider social values. It is when this tension becomes intolerable, for example in becoming a danger to others, that the social philosophy of individualism falls foul of the wider society taking action against him. In terms of the mentally disordered offender who is detained against his wishes and forced to have treatment, clearly the ethics of individualism are unsound.

2. Free will and determinism

These apparently opposed philosophical concepts govern our ideas on responsibility for one's own behaviour. Free will presupposes choice in all matters, which is clearly not absolute as there is much to life that we have little influence over. Similarly, determinism presupposes inevitability of cause and effect, which excludes choice of action. It would seem apparent that human action falls somewhere between these polarised philosophical ideas. For example, we may understand a degree of determinism which governs social action, as the culture to which we belong sets parameters on the ways in which we are expected to behave. Clearly, the socialisation process is a limitation on our free will but may not totally exclude some choice. The forensic patient within our secure psychiatric service has been considered to engage in the social action of his choice (however restricted that might be) and at the same time this has been theoretically determined by other events (command hallucinations, environmental upbringing). However, both society and the forensic practitioner makes judgements on the extent to which we believe the patient acts on his free will and defines his responsibility. Similarly, we make judgements regarding the extent to which his actions were determined by causally related events, which may exonerate him from such responsibility.

3. Autonomy

Autonomy is more than individualism and the use of free will. It is often described as having three central components: autonomy of thought, which incorporates action based on one's own decisions, mental assessments, preferences etc.; autonomy of will, which is the freedom to act on one's own deliberations; and autonomy of action, in which the exercise of the former can be implemented in practice. Gillon (1985) summarised autonomy as:

> seeing it as a virtue...in Aristotlian vein...on the one hand, the deficiency of heteronomy in which one is excessively influenced by others (for example, by being credulous, gullible, compliant, passive, submissive, overdependent, or servile) and, on the other hand, the excess of arrogant self sufficiency or even solipsism (various doctrines exhibiting a total concern with self).

The forensic patients are morally granted the right to be autonomous but with severe restrictions. Their autonomy of thought is curtailed through mind-altering drugs or 'talking therapies', their autonomy of will is restrained through prescribing limits to their behaviours, and their autonomy of action is confined by the rules of normative standards.

4. Beneficence and non-maleficence

Beneficence is concerned with the *practice* of allowing no harm to be inflicted, and removing and preventing harm to others. The emphasis is placed on actually doing good for others and not merely wishing to, believing it is better to, or feeling that we ought to, do good. However, it is clear that in practice the concept of 'the patient's interests always comes first' in relation to beneficence lacks substance, as Gillon (1985) noted: 'it takes only a few moments of reflection to see that this is certainly not true in practice and undesirable as a moral imperative'. Simply because one individual's, or group's, interests always comes first. Non-maleficence is a response to the practical difficulties of beneficence (and some would say not a very good one) and involves the notion of at least not causing harm to others. We can see that whilst we may not be able, in practice, to prevent harm to everyone, we can in principle not cause harm to others. However, there are also problems with this interpretation which involves the moral propriety of action over non-action, performing over granting, negative over positive, and common over uncommon means.

Society willingly accepts that its members should not be harmed and compulsory detention of mentally disordered offenders is the medicalised response when this occurs. Whereas prison may be viewed as retribution, or justice, in terms of making amends to society with the loss of liberty, compulsory detention for treatment salves the social conscience when such an offender is considered 'ill'. However, such disposal in the form of compulsory detention and obligatory treatment can be interpreted as non-beneficent and actually maleficent for the patients concerned.

5. Utilitarianism

Utilitarianism is a normative ethical doctrine that attempts to explain right and wrong. At its simplest it is commonly understood as 'the greatest happiness for the greatest number', and although this appears as a most persuasive moral philosophy it is fraught with dangers. It is worth stating here that utilitarianism is sub-divided into two variants: act utilitarianism and rule utilitarianism. In the former the concern is with the appropriateness of each individual action being assessed on the results it produces, which is commonly understood as 'the ends justify the means'. In the latter, the idea is to do what would be prescribed by the optimum set of rules if they were obediently carried out, which is commonly known as 'always tell the truth'. Clearly, as mentioned above, both are fraught with dangers. It would appear that society readily engages in the utilitarian ethic in relation to the mentally disordered offender.

> The greatest happiness for the greatest number (i.e. society) formulates a series of socially constructed images that underscore the legislative legitimation of compulsory detention and forced treatment of dangerous individuals. These images involve the medicalisation of the criminal, with madness and badness interchangeably employed within the notion of 'sickness'. This cradles both 'sickness' and 'sin' in a complex social semantic encompassing notions of difference, divergence and deviance. The mentally disordered offender *becomes* the 'dangerous individual'. (Foucault 1978)

In utilitarian terms this allows for all manner of justified, albeit cushioned, actions for the ultimate protection of society.

6. Paternalism

Paternalism is a term that denotes the father–child analogy and has an intricate web of both positive and negative values. It is sometimes understood to have a dominant–submissive relationship whilst at other times it is seen as the power to protect and control in return for loyalty and obedience. Max Weber (1922) saw it, at a societal level, as traditional political authority in which subjects are regulated by the organisation of economically productive units both agricultural and industrial. Paternalism is said to possess five basic features: (a) dependency, in which the subordinate does not have access to power and resources; (b) ideological subordination within the caring role; (c) subject co-operativeness, in which the social organisation treats all subordinates collectively; (d) systematisation and institutionalisation, as it becomes part of the organised rule formation; and (e) diffused relationships, covering all aspects of subordinates' life.

Compulsory detention and forced treatment of mentally disordered offenders can be seen as a paternalistic system fulfilling all five features above. Forensic psychiatry and its paternal agents operate an organisation which necessarily produces a dependency by subordination within a 'caring role'. The organised unit treats all subordinates alike in terms of rules and governs all aspects of their lives. Within a totalising concept of paternalism, power and resources are removed from the patient and his personal control is diminished. The system always 'knows best' and knows what is best for the subordinates, just as the parent does for the child. A line of argument that is commonly used in forensic practice is 'it is not in the patient's best interests', this being rooted in the paternalistic ethic.

7. Idealism

Idealism is here referred to as a description of social reality through the everyday interactions and subjectivity of the social actors. It is based in both the personally and socially highly valued goals, and the attempts to achieve them. Idealism goes beyond the popular notion of ideal as answering to one's own highest conception of what is best and adds the quality of explanation of a social reality. Forensic practitioners employ socially constructed notions of 'dangerousness' as a medicalised concept to reinforce the notion of patient as patient, rather than criminal. Through the ethic of idealism they are then governed from the values of the treatment ethic which is considered to possess explanatory powers, the efficacy of remedy, and the accuracy of prognosis (Mason and Mercer 1998). The active role of social actors in the forensic domain is the construction of a social reality which perpetuates dangerousness as a clinical entity susceptible to the 'science' of psychiatry (Mason and Mercer 1999).

In concluding this section it would appear that forensic mental health care practitioners face considerable ethical difficulties and, although undertaken with the best of intentions, dilemmas remain. It is possible to argue that three of the philosophical positions, utilitarianism, paternalism and idealism, may have an appeal to those working with mentally disordered offenders. However, many practitioners in this setting may well be uncomfortable with these value theories. It would not be surprising to find that undertaking research on the multi-disciplinary groups involved in the forensic mental health care causes alarm in practitioners. The 'fear of scrutiny' is all too apparent.

MULTI-DISCIPLINARY OBSTACLES AND HURDLES IN FORENSIC RESEARCH

Here the focus is on systemic structures within an organisational framework in which professionals engage. This will be undertaken by employing Lee's (1993) 'research as threat' typology and highlighting examples from research practice, which will also incorporate both obstructions to research and strategies for overcoming them.

Research as threat

When research is considered by individuals to be threatening, either to the vested interests of individuals or organisations, then obstructions to that research may be undertaken, despite this being unethical. It should be remembered that organisations, and the many committees that constitute them, do not actually exist; it is the human beings that operate them that do. Furthermore, although we are all socialised into the particular cultural mosaic that represents our society, we are also socialised into the particular professional ideology representative of our chosen career groups. This can, and does, raise inter-disciplinary conflicts and tensions.

1. Intrusive threat

If it is accepted that as an emerging profession forensic practice must prove its worth to society in order for it to sustain the argument for its continuance, then scrutiny of its practice is required. However, there may be many professionals working in forensic mental health who would consider an investigation into their practice as threatening. The number of inquiries across the special hospitals as well as numerous medium secure units would indicate some elements of bad practice were developed. Those accounting for these bad practices would clearly see research as threatening. However, at a multi-disciplinary level there may be others who are not directly involved in the bad practices but are guilty by association or through line manager accountability. Even if we suggest that bad practices have been eliminated from the forensic domain and no longer exist we are left with the question as to whether good practices have replaced them. If much of forensic practice is related to mere containment then such 'warehousing' will be geared towards maintaining control (Mason 1999). Research into these strategies would also be threatening to both individuals and organisations who are attempting to offer the public image of health care. However, those workers engaged in good practices of mental health care delivery are unlikely to feel threatened by research unless they consider the efficacy of their practice as insufficient.

Individuals who wish to create obstruction to research that is considered threatening can simply decline to volunteer and little can, or should, be done to persuade involvement. However, as was stated above, the concern here is not at an individual level but at a systems level. The main concern revolves around the cultural formation of groups within forensic domains. General psychiatric ward cultures have received some research attention with the predominant themes indicating that they can become closed, insular and abusive (Goffman 1961; Morrison 1990). Forensic psychiatric ward cultures have been discussed by Richman and Mason (1992) who identified several layers of nursing operations on the wards in order to produce a professional façade. Furthermore, Richman (1998) found one ward in a special hospital to be a 'tinderbox' of power dynamics and on the verge of erupting into violence. However, other than Richman's anthropo-logical work there has been little research undertaken and we are left with the reports from inquiries or anecdotes from personal experience. Most inquiry reports suggest that forensic cultures operate abusive strategies, which are consciously or unconsciously derived, but obviously the inquiry team focuses on the negative areas in which the allegations or concerns are laid. The catch-22 situation sums up the position aptly. We need good anthropological studies to be undertaken across forensic hospitals and units and yet the closed nature of these establishments excludes such research from being undertaken. Thus it would appear to be the responsibility of multi-disciplinary managers to commission and facilitate these researchers if they are serious in their quest to deliver quality services.

2. Threat of sanction
If forensic practitioners or forensic organisations feel that research findings may reveal something which may be used against them, then research may be obstructed. We must have serious questions to ask of those individuals and organisations regarding what it is that is creating such threat. It would appear that individuals themselves as practitioners or managers can see something that if revealed could be used against them. If this is the case then

it must be a cause for serious alarm and, more importantly, an area that needs to be changed.

Responsible Medical Officers (RMOs) may refuse to grant permission for patients in their charge to be involved in research using clinical grounds irrespective of whether this is the real reason. Multi-disciplinary groups may obstruct the research at various committee levels with all manner of arguments regarding the quality of the research, its usefulness or its scientific rigour. Many lines of argument are employed to hide the fact that it is the research, or the researcher, which is actually being obstructed. Although most forensic arenas now come under the Local Research Ethics Committee system, some, at the time of writing, do not. Forensic ethics committees may comprise individuals who might operate unethically in obstructing research which may be considered threatening. Some ethics committees in the forensic arena comprise individuals who may be unqualified in both medical ethics and philosophies of science, and merely operate to protect the organisation.

For example, in one health care setting where a research committee reviewed study protocols in order to assess scientific validity prior to consideration by the ethics committee, concern was expressed at the number of research proposals being rejected by the ethics committee. A research proposal was designed which aimed to investigate the reasons for this high rate of rejections from the ethics committee. The proposal was passed by the research committee and forwarded to the ethics committee. The minutes reveal that it never 'officially' arrived and a letter was received from the chief executive of the organisation, who did not sit on either of the committees mentioned. The letter stated that 'this organisation did not support such research and it must cease immediately'. Clearly, someone from either the research committee or the ethics committee had vested interests to protect and had taken the proposal 'unofficially' to the chief executive who, evidently, supported the obstructing of research to protect the organisation. The main point to note is the corruption of the organisational culture which can sustain such practices.

Strategies to overcome such obstructions include the need to reveal such practices and attempt to have them openly discussed. It is often the case that individuals are not under threat but only perceive themselves to be. Although policies and practices may be affected, many individuals fear change itself the most. Therefore, sharing information is a good starting point. However, if powerful members of committees and organisations are operating to obstruct research then two lines of advance can be undertaken. The first involves approaching successive lines of management regarding the matter until this is exhausted, and this approach has the impact of revealing to others one's concerns. The second is to inform Trust authorities and ultimately the Secretary of State for Health. However, be warned: these strategies carry career dangers for the researcher.

3. Political threat

Research in forensic health care which is considered as a political threat would appear to take on two broad forms. The first relates to politics in its widest sense, in that forensic psychiatry shares a close relationship with political departments in government frameworks such as the Home Office and Department of Health. The positive elements of this relationship are the day-to-day working of these political departments in relation to the business of the forensic hospitals, clinics and units. The negative connotations arise from the political concerns regarding such aspects as the reoffending of released patients and the situations that lead to both private and public inquiries. The second broad political threat relates to the power relations of the professions working within multi-disciplinary teams in forensic practice. Research that is considered a threat by certain professions may result in obstructions to certain types of investigations.

Forensic organisations are often said to be concerned with making decisions that must not 'embarrass the minister' and this includes strategies of censorship (Mason 1997). Research which may reveal information which, if published, may do so is clearly a political threat. As was noted above, it is human nature to protect one's vested interests and the boundaries between what is considered ethical and unethical decision making may become obfuscated, as the extreme example of the Nazi medical experiments have clearly shown (Lagerwey 1999). Human decisions made officially at committee levels, or unofficially in the 'canteen', to obstruct research that may be politically sensitive does occur and must be considered unethical in itself.

The second element of political threat, that of inter-professional power, is a serious obstacle to some research in the forensic arena. The majority of members of committees in this area, whether they be research, ethics or management committees, understandably arise from the professional groups that are involved in forensic practice. These will inevitably be psychiatry, psychology, social work, nursing and occupational therapy, to name the major groups. However, it is predominantly the former two professional groups of psychiatry and psychology that are considered the 'hard' sciences, the empirical positivists, and whose views are the most influential on 'scientific' matters. It is a commonly held view that their training in the empirical scientific method qualifies them on all matters pertaining to research generally. Of course, this is sophistry, but ensures that the power of their professional authority carries the most weight, particularly when the decision makers are less confident in their knowledge of research methodologies. Thus, some research in forensic psychiatry may be obstructed, particularly the qualitative scientific methodologies such as sociology, anthropology, ethnology, phenomenology and ethnomethodology, on the grounds that they may be considered methodologically weak, when in reality their methods and the scientific principles underpinning them are either not accepted or not understood. To be fair, the same obstructions can be applied to quantitative studies by qualitative researchers on the committees that they may dominate, and in either scenario must be considered unethical.

A third element to this political threat concerns individuals within professional groups who believe that only members of that professional group should research issues within that profession. For example, some nurses tend to believe that only nurses can research nursing issues, with the usual rationale being that only nurses would understand those issues. This, again, is sophistry. Professional groups like to circumscribe professional knowledge and when taken too far can obstruct others from engaging in research. There is no reason why any trained professional scientist cannot research the issues within another profession as long as the aims of the project are appropriate, the method is sound, and the individual's knowledge of analysis is appropriate.

To combat these obstructions, research and ethics committees in forensic practice ought to have a balanced membership from the wider scientific research arena. If this cannot be achieved then at least they ought to be able to access university departments in the appropriate branch of science in order to obtain expert feedback on the relative merits, or otherwise, of the research project being considered, by those specialising in that science. This will counteract the mere dismissal of other research by those whose particular methodological paradigm it does not fit. A second strategy to overcome this type of political threat is to engage in multi-disciplinary research which incorporates more than one method. Although this can create difficulties it can be effective in allowing each discipline to focus on its own approach without disrupting the overall research strategy. Multi-disciplinary research, multi-agency research and multi-site research is the preferred structure for many research funding bodies and will also help overcome the political threat in which one profession believes that a particular type or area of research is its domain only.

CONCLUSION

This chapter has attempted to draw a number of elements together to focus on multi-disciplinary aspects of researching forensic mental health issues. In concluding the chapter I would like to draw out some of the major points. First, multi-disciplinary working is a complex affair in which personal and professional ideologies could make the enterprise difficult. Second, Lee's (1993) typology is useful when considering the potential obstructions to research. Third, there are many different types of value theories operating within forensic health care and the multi-disciplinary team. This may be a source of tension within teams and further work is required in this area. Indeed, the entire domain of forensic practice would benefit from a closer ethical examination. Finally, there are levels of human operations that are geared towards protecting vested interests which reveal themselves despite professional discourse to the contrary. If the forensic profession is to convince society that it is a worthwhile endeavour then it urgently needs to engage in research that will highlight good practices and provide information to change bad ones.

SUMMARY

- Many different value theories inform forensic health care practice.
- In multi-disciplinary team working, the operation of multiple value theories can cause confusion or tension.
- Research in forensic health care settings, particularly that involving multi-disciplinary teams, will be sensitive research.

- A framework for understanding the potential threats posed by research is useful for all those involved and aids reflexive research practice.

- New developments in the organisational review and regulatory framework of research procedures seek to clarify the responsibilities of all parties involved in the research process. This may bring more transparency to the consideration of sensitive research.

REFERENCES

Appelbaum, P.S. (1997) 'A Theory of Ethics for Forensic Psychiatry.' *Journal of the American Academy of Psychiatry and Law 25*, 3, 233–246.

Berman, E. and Segel, R. (1982) 'The Captive Client: Dilemmas of Psychotherapy in the Psychiatric Hospital.' *Psychotherapy, Theory, Research and Practice*, 19, 31–41.

Bloch, S. and Chodoff, P. (1981) *Psychiatric Ethics*. Oxford: Oxford University Press.

Brewer, J.D. (1990) 'Sensitivity as a Problem in Field Research: A Study of Routine Policing in Northern Ireland.' *American Behavioral Scientist.* 33, 578–593.

Brooker, C. and Whyte, L. (2000) *Multidisciplinary Team Working in Secure Psychiatric Environments*. Report submitted to the high security psychiatric services commissioning board.

Cott, C. (1998) 'Structure and Meaning in Multi-disciplinary Teamwork.' *Sociology of Health and Illness 20*, 6, 848–873.

Drinka, T. and Ray, R. (1987) 'An Investigation of Power in an Interdisciplinary Health Care Team.' *Gerontology and Geriatric Education 6*, 3, 45–53.

Foucault, M. (1978) 'About the Concept of the "Dangerous Individual" in 19th Century Legal Psychiatry.' *International Journal of Law and Psychiatry 1*, 1, 1–18.

Gillon, R. (1985) *Philosophical Medical Ethics*. Chichester: John Wiley & Sons.

Goffman, I. (1961) *Asylums: Essays on the Social Situation of Mental Patients and Other Inmates*. London: Penguin.

Guzzo, R.A. and Shea, G.P. (1992) 'Group Performance and Intergroup Relations.' In L. Dunnette and M. Hough (eds) *Handbook of Industrial and Organisational Psychology*. Palo Alto: Consulting Psychologists Press.

Her Majesty's Stationery Office (1992) *Report of the Committee of Inquiry into Complaints about Ashworth Hospital*. London: HMSO.

Lagerwey, D.M. (1999) 'Nursing Ethics at Hadamer.' *Qualitative Health Research* 9, 6, 759–772.

Lee, R.M. (1993) *Doing Research on Sensitive Topics*. London: Sage.

Mason, T. (1997) 'Censorship of Research in the Health Service Setting.' *Nurse Researcher 4*, 4, 83–92.

Mason, T. (1999) 'The Psychiatric "Supermax?: Long-term High-security Psychiatric Services.' *International Journal of Law and Psychiatry 22*, 2, 155–166.

Mason, T. and Jennings, L. (1997) 'The Mental Health Act and Professional Hostage Taking.' *Journal of Medicine, Science and the Law 37*, 1, 58–68.

Mason, T. and Mercer, D. (1998) *Critical Perspectives in Forensic Care: Inside Out*. London: Macmillan.

Mason, T. and Mercer, D. (1999) *A Sociology of the Mentally Disordered Offender*. London: Longman.

McGrath, M. (1993) 'Whatever Happened to Teamwork?: Reflections on Community Mental Health Teams.' *British Journal of Social Work*, 23, 15–19.

Morrison, E. (1990) 'The Tradition of Toughness: A Study of Non-professional Nursing Care in Psychiatric Settings.' *Image: Journal of Nursing Scholarship 22*, 1, 32–38.

Moss, R. (1994) 'Community Mental Health Teams: A Developing Culture.' *Journal of Mental Health*, 3, 167–174.

National Health Service Executive (1993) *Nursing in Primary Health Care: New World, New Opportunities*. London: HMSO.

Payne, G., Dingwall, R., Payne, J. and Carter, M. (1980) *Sociology and Social Research*. London: Routledge and Kegan Paul.

Procter-Childs, T., Freeman, M. and Miller, C. (1998) 'Visions of Teamwork: The Realities of an Interdisciplinary Approach.' *British Journal of Therapy and Rehabilitation 5*, 12, 616–635.

Renzetti, C.M. and Lee, R.M. (1993) *Researching Sensitive Topics*. London: Sage.

Richman, J. (1998) 'The Ceremonial and Moral Order of a Ward for Psychopaths.' In T. Mason and D. Mercer (eds) *Critical Perspectives in Forensic Care: Inside Out*. London: Macmillan.

Richman, J. and Mason, T. (1992) 'Quo Vadis the Special Hospitals.' In S. Scott *et al.* (eds) *Private Risks and Public Dangers.* Aldershot: Averbury.

Roberts, P. and Priest, H. (1997) *Coaching Your Employees.* London: Kogan Page.

Rostocki, A. (1986) 'Sensitive Questions in Sociological Survey.' *Polish Sociological Bulletin,* 75, 27–32.

Sieber, J. and Stanley, B. (1988) 'Ethical and Professional Dimensions of Socially Sensitive Research.' *American Psychologist,* 43, 49–55.

Weber, M. (1922) *Methods in the Social Sciences.* London: Dawsons.

West, M. (1994) *Effective Teamwork.* Leicester: British Psychological Society.

West, M. (1999) 'Communication and Teamwork in Healthcare. *Nursing Times Research 4,* 1, 8–17.

Williams, R., Vivian-Byrne, S. and Mason, T. (2000) *Analysis of Multi-disciplinary Teams in a Medium Secure Unit.* Unpublished Report. Caswell Clinic, South Wales.

CHAPTER 7

Research Ethics Committees and Research in Forensic Psychiatry

Christine Brown and Gwen Adshead

INTRODUCTION

Researchers and Research Ethics Committees (RECs) can sometimes come into conflict. Researchers can perceive ethics committees as inconsistent, arbitrary, slow and obstructive. REC members may perceive researchers as impatient, and insufficiently concerned about the risks and harms to potential subjects. In this chapter, we wish to explore some of the conceptual issues that underlie these perceptions, and how they apply to forensic mental health research. We will argue that both researchers and RECs face extra difficulties in assessing harms and risks in forensic mental health research; we will also argue that the concept of autonomy, and the capacity to take research participation decisions, is more complicated in forensic settings.

BACKGROUND

Unlike the USA, where RECs are instituted by legislation, ethics committees in the UK have developed more informally. First proposals by the Royal College of Physicians were supported by the (then) Ministry of Health, which, in 1967, recommended the setting up of Research Ethics Committees by health authorities. Each District Health Authority was required by the Department of Health to set up and provide administrative support for Local Research Ethics Committees (LRECs), which would act as independent advisors to the authorities on the ethics of research proposals involving their patients. In 1997, to facilitate ethical procedures in studies involving multiple (five or more) LRECs, regional Multi-centre Research Ethics Committees (MRECs) were established. These committees have no legal (statutory) basis, but it is a matter of good practice for all proposals to be reviewed by an REC – partly to satisfy Department of Health service guidelines (Department of Health 1991), and research governance requirements (discussed in greater detail below), and partly because most funding bodies and journals require such review.

Research Ethics Committees are made up of a 'reasonable body of independent experts'; originally 8-12 people, drawn from both sexes, a wide range of age groups and representing different professionals. At least one member should be 'unconnected with health care'; current guidance suggests that the committee membership should include at least one member with statistical expertise (Foster 1997). The Committee is required to produce an annual report on its activities.

In theory committee members could be held liable for injury to subjects participating in research approved by them. Concerns about research practice were raised during the inquiries relating to Bristol, Alder Hey and North Staffordshire hospitals. The Griffiths Report (NHS Executive 2000) recommended a framework of 'research governance' that would foster good quality research as well as protecting the interests of the 'public' [sic]. In particular, it recommends training for members of LRECs and administrators, and increased accountability on the part of the Department of Health, Trusts and researchers. The report also raises the question of how best to obtain consent to research participation from potential participants at times of emotional and physical vulnerability.

THE ETHICAL ROLE OF RECS: WHAT ARE THEY MEANT TO BE DOING?

RECs have a dual role (Department of Health 1995). The Helsinki Declaration requires ethics committees overseeing research to protect participants from harm, and prioritise their wellbeing over 'the interests of science and society' (World Medical Association 1964). RECs should also 'facilitate ethically acceptable attempts to identify new and better treatments'.

Thus RECs are required to be engaged in ethical reasoning in the process of assessing a new proposal. In doing so, they attend to those parts of the proposal that speak to the legal and ethical rights of the participant: to not be put at risk, unless there is express and informed consent by the subject about the nature of the risks and possible benefits of the research. Horror at what had been done to prisoners of the Nazis in the name of medical research has resulted in a powerful emphasis on obtaining consent to participation by research subjects. Obtaining consent, in one sense, is a proxy for respect for the individual autonomy of each person, and his claim to be treated as a unique human being, who is an agent in his own right, and not (in Kant's famous phrase) 'merely a means to an end' (1998, p.181). Regulation of disclosure of private information obtained in the context of research is also a proxy for this type of human respect.

The ethical considerations also include a careful assessment of the risks and benefits, and attention to the welfare of the subject. The Helsinki Declaration states that medical research 'is only justified if there is a reasonable chance that the population in which the research is carried out stand to benefit from the results', and that RECs are required to ensure that the study makes a minimal impact on the subject's health: physical, mental and personality (World Medical Association 1964).

RECs, it seems, will not allow participants to choose to put themselves at any significant level of risk, even if they have consented to it. One difficulty faced by RECs relates to perception of risks and benefits, and how to weigh up the impact of future events that may not happen. Researchers, REC members and potential subjects may perceive risks and benefits differently, and weigh up their likelihood in different ways. Different stakeholders in the research process may also perceive risks and benefits that others may not see; for example, incarcerated subjects may perceive a benefit to research participation, through their compliance, that no amount of information to the contrary may dispel.

In addition to considering the ethical justification for the research, there is some question about the extent to which RECs are invited or required to assess the scientific validity of a project. Clearly, scientifically invalid research cannot be ethically justified, since it may put participants at risk to no purpose; this was one aspect of the Nazi research programme which led to the condemnation of doctors involved in that research at the later medical trials.

However, this concern can sometimes mean that RECs are looking at the *scientific* value of a research proposal, as opposed to its *moral* value.

Different types of value-based reasoning are therefore called for. An interesting twist to this process is the argument that unethically justifiable research is unscientific – that something about its moral value, in terms of dignity and respect, gives meaning to its quantitative value (*JME* Dachau debate as mentioned in Angell 1992, p.276–285).

CONCERNS ABOUT RECS

There has been increasing research interest into the function and reasoning processes of RECs themselves. Several studies have suggested that RECs come to inconsistent conclusions, so that the same proposal can result in different responses (Alberti 1995, 2000; Gilbert, Fulford and Parker 1989). Whether this is really inconsistency is debatable; a claim to consistency could imply that there is a universal 'right' response, which RECs ought to be able to achieve. Such research may reflect a positivistic bias on the part of the researchers – a positivistic bias which exists in medicine generally. The fact that RECs give different answers suggests that different groups of people may analyse values in different ways, and weigh them differently. One group may privilege welfare, another scientific validity. The group members will influence such group processes; a REC with user representation may come to a different conclusion about a project than one that does not.

What might be more informative is more information about the decision making processes, and the ways that RECs reason, rather than a simple focus on outcome. What we want to know is whether the REC has made a good quality decision, is self-reflective about bias, properly informed, capable of taking multiple perspectives etc. These are some of the elements of ethical reasoning skills (Fulford *et al.* 1995) and we do not know if REC members possess these skills, or even are aware that they need them. Such skills are particularly necessary in mental health, where there is often much more uncertainty about some of the major conceptual issues, and value judgements are an essential part of diagnosis and therapy (Fulford 1989).

In 1994 the Department of Health introduced a standards initiative for training REC members, which was concerned with concepts of quality assurance and improvement to research ethics. Some academic centres (such as King's College, London) run training courses for members of RECs, especially in relation to psychiatric research. The Griffiths Report (NHS

Executive 2000) also emphasised the importance of training LREC members; however, it makes no mention of the type of reasoning skills that members might need.

All the same concerns could be applied to psychiatric researchers. Few researchers (especially the most senior) will have had any exposure to the teaching and training in bioethics that is now mandatory in medical school curricula. They are likely to be subject to sources of bias of which they are unaware: beliefs that welfare holds greater value than autonomy, that scientific knowledge has a greater value than other benefits, and (perhaps most commonly) that, because they are scientists, they operate in a value-free way, and their judgements are either beneficial or value-neutral. Full-time researchers may have had little contact with users of mental health services, and their communication skills (an essential part of ethical reasoning) may be poor. Lastly, they may find it hard to factor into the ethical process that they themselves stand to gain most in the short term if the research project is accepted by the REC, since researchers' personal careers are advanced by getting grants and publishing completed research, both of which need REC approval (Bartlett 1995; Brown 2002).

SPECIAL ETHICAL DILEMMAS FOR RECS
AND FORENSIC MENTAL HEALTH

In this section, we describe some particular ethical dilemmas for RECs considering forensic mental health projects.

1. How should RECs decide between competing values? This is an old problem in moral philosophy, and there is no easy answer. Attention to consequences is part of the solution; clearly a value judgement that results in more harm than good is not going to be ethically justifiable.

However, most dilemmas are not like this. Conflicts between REC members can arise because there is diversity of values, without a structure for thinking about how to negotiate the conflict. Social values may be confused with ethical values or clinical values; not all of these will be synonymous. This is particularly so in forensic settings, where RECs may feel that they need to address themselves to public safety or institutional security issues, even though these hardly fit into the Helsinki remit. Acknowledging diversity results in richer argument, but can also cause anxiety and even anger.

2.   The assessment of risk and benefit of a research procedure may be particularly difficult in respect of subjects who themselves have been a source of risk and harm to others. It is possible for there to be confusion about the different types of harm and to whom RECs owe an ethical (if not legal) duty of care. The Helsinki Declaration specifically states that the interests of subjects outweigh social interests (World Medical Association 1964); it is hard to see how this principle can operate in settings where society's interests routinely outweigh those of the subjects. Vulnerable subjects are usually given extra protection and extra claims to rights rather than less; will such a position be tenable in forensic mental health, where subjects are stigmatised and deprived of rights in the name of public safety?

The other problem here is that RECs are really being invited to carry out a risk assessment of the project – but, like all risk assessments, this can include consideration of any harm that the REC members can imagine, whether probable or not. Indeed, the probability of harm is sometimes the subject of the research protocol in itself. Not all imagined consequences are meaningful; it is just as difficult to assess the reliability and validity of the REC's risk assessment as any other risk assessment.

3.   Department of Health guidance on research applies to *patients*, past and present. However, not all potential forensic research subjects are patients. Serving or remand prisoners are not patients (unless housed in prison hospital settings); individuals who are being evaluated for court hearings are arguably clients, rather than patients. The nature of the relationship between forensic assessors and those they assess remains the subject of ethical debate (Candilis *et al.* 2001); how much more so if the evaluation itself becomes the subject of research. The nature of the relationship to some extent delineates the ethical duty.

Patients arguably deserve increased protection because they may be made less competent by their medical conditions, apart from the question of their dependence on the health care professionals around them. Should the criteria for competence to consent to research be higher or lower for non-patients, who may be vulnerable in other ways? In English law, the legal test of competence to consent to *treatment* is stated in *Re C* (1994). Whether this can be applied to research, given the different purposes and interests of the players involved, is debatable (see Chapter 1). Could there be different standards of competence to volunteers, subjects and participants, and how can we choose between them?

4.   The assessment of competence of forensic subjects to consent to research may be problematic for a number of reasons. Most research bodies acknowledge the vulnerability of potential research subjects who are detained against their will. Forensic psychiatric subjects may be seen paradoxically as both especially vulnerable (because ill and detained) but also as especially dangerous and untrustworthy. Recognising the autonomy of detained persons may be as important as recognising their lack of autonomy. The Helsinki Declaration states that subjects must be volunteers and informed participants (World Medical Association 1964, Section 20); to what extent can forensic institutions allow detainees to be informed volunteers? Many researchers speak of LRECs that refuse to allow potential subjects to be even asked about research participation; where does proper concern for vulnerable subjects become a type of paternalistic intrusion that demeans the choices of potential subjects? There is in fact some evidence that detention, *per se*, has little effect on the capacity to make research decisions, but that the communication skills of the researcher does have some effect (Appelbaum *et al.* 1987).

5.   The problem of consent is particularly acute in forensic research because so much is non-therapeutic in nature, i.e. there is no direct benefit to the research subjects themselves. Indeed, in forensic research, there may be no benefit to the research population *at all*, either now or in the future. The proposed benefit is often couched in terms of reducing the risk that the subjects pose to others in the future, so that the only direct benefit to the subjects may be that they will not be risky to others. This can hardly be said to be a *health* benefit, specific to forensic patients; it looks more like a

social or moral benefit, which might be applied to any citizen. Further, to carry out non-therapeutic research, which does not benefit the proposed subject group, is contrary to Section 19 of the Helsinki Declaration (World Medical Association 1964).

The other ethical aspect of non-therapeutic research relates to competence to consent. Given that non-therapeutic research carries no benefit, and may even carry some burden or risk, it seems plausible to argue that the threshold for competence to consent might be set higher than for treatment decisions. Although few forensic patients will be so incapacitated by their illnesses that they lack capacity, some will not be competent (those with treatment resistant psychosis, for example). The guidelines from most reputable bodies on non-therapeutic research with incompetent subjects clearly state that such research, involving incompetent subjects, must be to the benefit of that group. However, the only identifying research factor of the group is not a feature of their *medical* condition, but their *social* condition, i.e. that they are offenders. There is no reason to carry out research into a condition of forensic patients unless it contributes in some way to their forensic status, which is not a biomedical issue.

6.   A particularly contentious area for RECs relates to the issue of rewards and inducements. Most research guidelines from established bodies recommend that subjects should be reimbursed for time and effort, although this should not be excessive. There is recognition of the fact that much research with healthy volunteers is unlikely to take place without some reward; indeed, this is consistent with the economic value systems of the Western cultures that carry out most research. There is also an acknowledgement that rewards should not be so great as to induce the vulnerable to put themselves at risk.

This tension between rewards and inducements is complicated enough in general research settings, such as pharmaceutical company research. In forensic contexts, it becomes even more complicated. Some RECs have taken the view that any monetary reward would be a reward for past crime – a view that received some support in the press response to the payment of Mary Bell for her participation in a published biography (Brown 2002). Although monetary reward might be seen as an inducement (especially where there are few other opportunities for detained patients to earn money), the other concern expressed by most research bodies is that subjects may think that compliance with research will bring benefits in terms of reduced detention or advanced release. Given that most detainees are held in social systems where compliance usually does have an important effect on release date, this is hardly surprising. It may be hard to persuade subjects that this is not the case, when we know that ordinary hospital patients may not be able to tell the difference between treatment and research (Appelbaum *et al.* 1987).

7.   Risk assessment research has special problems (some discussed by Logan in Chapter 5). What is it that research participants are consenting to? The 'risks' that potential subjects may be exposed to include the risk that they will be detected in offending earlier, or may incriminate themselves without being aware of doing so. Longitudinal follow-up studies of risky patients provides good quality data, but perhaps at a cost to privacy. There is an interesting conflict here in current Department of Health policy; on the one hand, research subjects will have to give express consent to disclosure of research material except in certain cases, usually where they cannot be identified. However, risks assessment research relies on identifiable follow-up, and risk to self or others may subject to mandatory disclosure under proposed changes to mental health legislation. Indeed, medical confidentiality is already trumped by risk where there is danger to an identifiable person (as indicated by the judgements in *Egdell* and *Palmer*). Where will the consent to the risk research participant to disclosure fit in? How does the advice about user views and involvement in research apply to forensic patients?

8.   The traditional biomedical disease focus in research means lack of consideration of ethical issues raised by disability and living with disability. Where there is long-term dependence, there may be different conceptions of autonomy and consent (Agich 1990). This is likely to apply to residents of long-term forensic institutions where people are not only detained; they are, in some sense, at home. Relationships with staff are a complex mixture of coercion and care, and this may affect who obtains consent from

potential research participants, and how. Many research bodies suggest that clinical relationships and research relationships should be kept separate, and some suggest that clinicians should obtain consent from patients, rather than researchers who may be biased towards persuading the patient to participate. However, in forensic settings, the clinician may be not be seen in a benevolent light by the patient, and may not perceive either the doctors or nurses to have his best interests at heart. Alternatively, the pressure to comply with clinicians' suggestions may be greater than for researchers. It may also be difficult to assess possible distress to subjects who are already in a state of chronic distress, in terms of their remorse, regret and social exclusion.

CONCLUSION

It would probably be of help to have more information about how potential research participants in forensic settings see research processes, and understand their part in it. However, this raises the interesting question about the capacity to consent to research on capacity, especially in vulnerable subjects. It may be that greater attention to user views in medical research could justify using different methodologies to explore these issues, especially drawing on methods from social science. As several authors in our book have noted, one problem with the traditional biomedical approach to research, and research ethics, is that it is always in danger of ignoring the social context of the research. This danger is partly what the Declaration of Helsinki was drafted to address (World Medical Association 1964).

This must be particularly true of forensic subjects who are largely defined socially as offenders, and this is part of their psychological 'problem'. Perhaps the most difficult aspect is that of letting the forensic subjects' voices be heard, especially when their voices are often dismissed as mad, bad or essentially false. If we want to get better information about forensic patients, and their mental conditions, we are going to have to find new ways of establishing a research narrative that will make sense both to the potential subject and the researcher.

REFERENCES

Agich, G. (1990) *Autonomy in Long-term Care.* Oxford: OUP.

Alberti, K.G.M. (1995) 'Local Research Ethics Committees.' *British Medical Journal,* 311, 639–640.

Alberti, K.G.M. (2000) 'Multicentre Research Ethics Committees: Has the Cure been worse than the Disease?' *BMJ 320,* 1157–1158.

Angell, M. (1992) 'Editorial Responsibility: Protecting Human Rights by Restricting Publication of Unethical Research.' In G. J. Anna and M. A. Grodin (eds) *The Nazi Doctors and the Nuremberg Code: Human Rights and Human Experimentation.* New York: Oxford University Press.

Appelbaum, P.S., Roth, L., Lidz, C., Benson, P. and Winslade, W. (1987) 'False Hopes and Best Data: Consent to Research and the Therapeutic Misconception.' Hastings Center Report (April) 20–24.

Bartlett, A. (1995) 'Ethics and Psychiatric Research.' *Psychiatric Bulletin,* 19, 670–672.

Brown, C. (2002) 'Entering Secure Psychiatric Settings.' In N. Rapport (ed) *British Subjects: An Anthropology of Britain.* Oxford: Berg, 223–238.

Candilis, P.J, Martinez, R. and Dording, C. (2001) 'Principles and Narrative in Forensic Psychiatry: Towards a Robust view of Professional Role.' *Journal of the American Academy of Psychiatry, Law 29,* 2, 167–173.

Convention on Human Rights and Biomedicine (2001) *Draft Additional Protocol on Biomedical Research.* Strasbourg: Council of Europe.

Department of Health (1991) *Local Ethics Committees.* London: Department of Health (HSG (91))5.

Department of Health (1994) *Standards for Local Research Ethics Committees – A Framework for Ethical Review.* London: Department of Health/NHSTD.

Department of Health (1995) *Briefing Pack for Research Ethics Committee Members.* London: Department of Health.

Department of Health (2001a) *Governance Arrangements for NHS Research Ethics Committees.* London: Department of Health, Central Office for Research Ethics Committees.

Department of Health (2001b) *Research Governance Framework for Health and Social Care.* London: Department of Health. www.doh.gov.uk/research/rd3/nhsrandd.

Fulford, K.W.M. (1989) *Moral Theory and Medical Practice.* Cambridge: Cambridge University Press.

Fulford, K.W.M., Ersser, S., Hope, R.A. and Hope, T. (1995) *Essential Practice Skills in Patient Centered Care*. Oxford: Blackwells.

Foster, C. (ed) (1997) *Manual for Research Ethics Committees*. (5th edition) London: Centre of Medical Law and Ethics, King's College.

Gilbert, C., Fulford, K.W. and Parker, C. (1989) 'Diversity in the Practice of District Ethics Committees.' *British Medical Journal*, 299, 1437–1439.

Kant, I. (1998) 'Duty and Categorical Rules.' In J. Sterba (ed) *Ethics: The Big Questions*. Oxford: Blackwell.

Medical Research Council (1991) *The Ethical Conduct of Research on the Mentally Incapacitated*. London: MRC.

Mental Health Act Commission (1997) *Research Involving Detained Patients*. London: MHAC, Position Paper 1.

NHS Executive West Midland Regional Office (2000) *Report of a Review of the Research Framework in North Staffordshire Hospital NHS Trust* (Chairman: Professor R. Griffiths). Leeds: NHS Executive.

Royal College of Psychiatrists (2000) *Guidelines for Researchers and for Research Ethics Committees on Psychiatric Research Involving Human Participants*. London: Royal College of Psychiatrists.

Savalescu, J. (2002) 'Two Deaths and Two Lessons: Is it Time to Review the Structure and Function of Research Ethics Committees?' *Journal of Medical Ethics*, 28, 37–40.

World Medical Association (1964) *Declaration of Helsinki: Ethical Principles for Medical Research Involving Human Subjects*. Helsinki: WMA. Amended 1975 (Tokyo), 1983 (Venice), 1989 (Hong Kong), 1996 (SA) and 2000 (Edinburgh).

CASES:

Re C (Adult: Refusal of Medical Treatment) [1994] 1 All ER 819.

R. v. Palmer.

W. v. Egdell [1990] 1 All ER 835.

CHAPTER 8

Doing Research on Sexual Health Within a Secure Environment

Jean Ruane

INTRODUCTION

This chapter is a story about how I tried to gain access to carry out research in a forensic setting. Rather than write an abstract and theoretical account of this, I decided that the reader would find the 'real life' commentary more engaging. I also think it vital that those who research in this field are clear and straightforward about reporting their experiences, both positive and negative. In my view only then can past experiences be used meaningfully in order to progress research on sensitive topics – the subject in this case being sexual health within a secure environment.

CONTEXT

When I use the term 'sexual health', I am referring to it in its broadest context, including biological, social and legal perspectives. To place the origin of the study in context, it is worth noting that seven years of experience as a forensic mental health nurse acted as the impetus for my research interest.

Within forensic settings, the psychosocial histories of many mentally disordered offenders are such that aspects of their sexual health become clinical rehabilitation priorities. There are patients that have both perpetrated sexual offences and those who have been victims of sexual offences (Taylor 1998). In addition, long-term in-patients continue to have the right to form and maintain intimate relationships, which may entail sexual activity (Gostin 2000). These activities may be overt or covert. If covert, patients are vulnerable to infection or unwanted pregnancy. Patients may also be involved in sexual exploitation, abuse and blackmail, as either victim or perpetrator (SHSA 1992; Swan and Taylor 1999). Clearly, forensic mental health practitioners need to be skilled and competent in terms of integrating patients' sexual health needs within assessment, rehabilitation, and health promotion and education strategies.

The forensic mental health literature reveals a dearth of studies about general sexual health matters, especially within the context of secure environments (Davidson 1999; Rae 1993; SHSA 1992; Swan and Taylor 1999). Following a review of relevant literature it became apparent that most previous studies (outside forensic settings) had acknowledged limitations in clinical practice. Thus far research has concentrated largely on measuring clinicians' personal attitudes towards sexuality, knowledge of sexuality and the relationship of these variables with clinical practice behaviours. Despite similarities in methods, research instrumentation and sampling, clear and consistent findings proved elusive. Concurring with Gamel, Davis and Hengeveld (1993), a gap in the literature was identified: clinicians' personal attitudes and perceptions of their professional responsibilities about patient sexuality had not been explored.

THE STUDY

I originally proposed an exploratory study using grounded theory methodology (Glaser 1992; Glaser and Strauss 1967) in order to examine:

1.   how forensic mental health staff perceived patients' sexual health needs

2.   how they perceived their role and function in relation to patients' sexual health.

The study was also designed to explore the influences upon staff practices, decision making and the factors affecting the incorporation of sexual health into individualised care strategies.

A single forensic psychiatric organisation was to be the research setting. All qualified staff from the disciplines of nursing, occupational therapy, social work, medicine and psychology were to be given an invitation to participate. In this way no professional group would be excluded. In order to explore the topic in depth, multiple data collection methods were chosen which were designed to complement each other and in some degree compensate for their respective strengths and weaknesses. The methods chosen were in-depth interviews, focus groups and a documentary analysis of relevant organisational policies and patient care notes. The overarching design and rationale for the study was based on interpretive rather than hypothetical-deductive principles. The study was therefore firmly rooted within the qualitative research paradigm (Silverman 2001).

PRELIMINARY CONCERNS

It can be argued that a researcher should not propose ideas that he believes unlikely to be supported or funded. Taken to its extreme, this view would result in any unpopular or sensitive research being neglected, which might result in areas requiring the most urgent or pressing attention being given less priority or publicity. This notion is not new and the dilemmas and complexities to be faced by those who wish to research the controversial are recognised by many. However, I would agree with Sieber and Stanley (1988, p.55) who argue: '...shying away from controversial topics, simply because they are controversial, is also an avoidance of responsibility'.

This is not to say that I was acting purely altruistically. I envisaged difficulties but continued, not just because I felt the study was relevant and justifiable, but also because I had maintained a strong interest in this field of practice over many years. These were my choices.

I was conscious from the beginning that I needed to design the study in a manner that would address organisational concerns. It was imperative that the research design took into account the perspectives of the managers and clinicians and the likely resistance to the study if their confidence could not be gained. It is clear that factors other than ethical or scientific merit can help or hinder the progress of research. This is especially true for research identified as 'sensitive', a term which can be hard to define. Sieber and Stanley (1988) have argued that sensitive research studies are those that have direct or indirect consequences for participants of the research. Lee (1993) and Renzetti and Lee (1993) have attempted a less ambiguous definition. For them, sensitive research is that which potentially poses a substantial *threat* to those who are or have been involved in it and this includes the researcher. What actually counts as 'substantial' is not discussed but the types of threat deemed to make research sensitive fall into three categories:

- intrusive threat
- threat of sanction
- political threat.

Intrusive threat

According to Lee (1993), intrusive threats are posed when research delves into the private, sacred or stressful. Although research into an individual's sexual health could be deemed 'private', the proposed study was not aiming to explore the sexual health of staff but their perceptions of their patients' sexual health needs and related clinical decisions and practices based on their practice experiences.

However, just because sexual health can be a legitimate clinical concern does not mean it will automatically be discussed in the clinical arena openly and without difficulty. The nature of the proposed study may have been perceived as an intrusive threat because it dealt with an area that is often emotionally charged and subject to complex social rules and cultural taboos. Discussion about sexual matters can be associated for some with feelings of shame and embarrassment. Talking about the sexuality and offending behaviour of patients can be distressing, especially when elements of sexual exploitation are involved. Staff in forensic settings may experience feelings of revulsion and abhorrence in relation to their patients' past histories, no matter what their level of professional training.

Threat of sanction

The study also had potential to be perceived as a threat in so far as it was patient-centred. The introduction of a patient-oriented culture has been difficult for many forensic staff to accept. In high secure or penal settings patient-centredness can be perceived as losing the balance between custody and therapy (Kaye and Franey 1999). Interviews with staff about their perceptions of and attitudes to patients' sexual health has the potential to uncover attitudes and activities which may be contrary to those underpinning contemporary professional health care values and philosophies. Some staff may be aware that their views and practices could conflict with policy and political rhetoric and fear reprisals if identified. From this it would not be unreasonable to assume that a number of staff would wish to avoid participation in the study. Others might be willing participants but might feel compelled to moderate their contributions for fear of incriminating themselves or others. One great hurdle was therefore going to be about winning the trust and confidence of the individuals who would be invited to participate so that full and frank accounts could be obtained. Additionally, there may be those who, during participation, reveal material with the potential to embarrass the organisation. Thus, before individuals could be approached, the permission and confidence of the organisation also had to be won. This was to be another hurdle to be faced and leads to the consideration of political threat.

Political threat

Political threat occurs when the researcher's presence and/or findings are viewed as threatening to the alignments, interests or security of the political culture of the organisation or context under study (Lee 1993). It might be argued that all research has potential to pose political threat because of the wider social context in which it takes place. However, the extent to which the proposed research could pose a political threat was greater in this case because of the nature of the clinical context under study.

Mentally disordered offenders do not tend to have the sympathetic support of the general public. They are stigmatised and perceived as posing two great risks to others: the risk of mental disorder, and the risk of violence (Markham 2000; Symonds 1998). Political systems have an interest in controlling those deemed to be a risk to public safety. Indeed there is valuable political capital to be made out of doing this both successfully and punitively. For example, some aspects of forensic mental health practice have been depicted as harsh and abusive (Blom-Cooper et al. 1992) but also liberal to excess (Fallon et al. 1999). In each of these cases forensic organisations had to undergo vast changes in order to rectify the perceived limitations. This illustrates that, in socio-political terms, forensic mental health organisations reside between a rock and a hard place. Whether or not their staff practise in accordance with current NHS expectations, the organisations have no guarantee that they will be judged sympathetically by the public, the press or by politicians. The organisations and the staff working within them constantly run the gauntlet of being criticised not only by the public but also by colleagues in other areas of health care. This has direct relevance to the proposed study.

The study could have determined that staff successfully assist patients in initiating and maintaining intimate relationships. Depending upon how such results were communicated and by whom, the general public may not view this as a positive aspect of forensic mental health care. Under a banner of 'liberal to excess', it could be used against the staff and the organisations in which they work. Alternatively, the proposed study may find that staff perceived patients' sexual health as a low priority, or discriminated within their practice. Under a banner of 'harsh and abusive', the potential is created to produce serious political backlashes at local and national levels. Either way, as Markham (2000) notes, there is a paradox between public opinion and policy as well as a contradiction of views expressed in public opinion itself. Organisations and clinicians, as implementers of policy, can be caught in the middle, vulnerable to criticism and ridicule. In this position they are well placed to be apportioned blame and thus become victims of the dominant discourse of the time. These are potentially serious threats.

MINIMISING THREAT: THE ORGANISATION

The literature emphasises that access to organisations is best secured and maintained by winning the confidence of lead individuals within them (Marshall and Rossman 1999; Morse and Field 1996; Seiber 1993). In a forensic organisation individuals with influence are to be found at many different levels and with many different and possibly opposing agendas. Support from one group of individuals is no guarantee of support from them all. From this it seemed a sensible decision to gain support for the study on a number of levels within the chosen organisation.

First I explored internal sources of support and advice within the organisation. I made use of existing relationships via individuals who had known me as a clinician. I successfully engaged with four senior clinicians and managers to make working relationships which included them in the process of supervision, consultation and representation of the research. Local and national representatives of staff organisations were also approached and they too gave support to the study. In addition to building a network of support within the organisation, I tried to make clear my commitment to transparency of purpose, process and outcome. It was emphasised that the study was about identifying best practice and looking for ways to make that happen. I made it clear how the material would be disseminated within the organisation, and how the organisation would have a part in the ownership of any published data.

External support for the study was also secured. This came in the form of Department of Health funding and from my employer who facilitated my release from other responsibilities to enable me to undertake the research on a full-time basis. In addition the study was endorsed and supported by the necessary academic faculties and committees within the host university.

Minimising intrusive threat: staff issues

I was concerned that as a person attached to a university and the Department of Health, I would be perceived by staff not only as distant from them but also threatening to them. There was absolutely no reason why staff should automatically trust me enough to engage in a research interview and furnish me with frank, sensitive information about themselves, their clinical practices and the patient group for which they cared. This kind of trust had to be earned; without it the study would be severely limited.

With this in mind I proposed that once the study had been granted ethical approval I would base myself at the study site for six months prior to commencing formal data collection procedures. During this time I planned to publicise the research within the organisation, and arrange formal and informal meetings with managers and practitioners in order to discuss the project. In this way all staff would have opportunities to understand the study and my role and function within it, without having to commit themselves to participation. These measures would also allow me to become a familiar face within the clinical setting. I hoped that this would enable staff to make their own judgements about my motives and whether or not I was a person to whom they would wish to divulge information. As Edwards (1993) demonstrates, this can make for a sense of some affinity between the researcher and the researched and is crucial in order to establish trust.

This approach also allowed me as a researcher to demonstrate an awareness, respect and sensitivity to the risk factors perceived by the potential participants. Seiber (1993) describes this as being 'culturally sensitive' and as highly relevant to successful ethical conduct within the research setting. With this in mind, participants were given choices about what aspect of the data collection methods they participated in, such as group or individual interviews, recording of interviews and having a copy of the interview transcript in order to make changes if they so wished. The latter point is of particular importance in dealing with 'delusions of alliance' (Stacey 1988), in which participants reveal more than they intend, and in facilitating 'member checks' (Rodgers 1999), where findings are discussed with participants to make sure that their contributions are accurately represented. In these ways the study sought to maximise interaction and afford participants a greater degree of control (Bergen 1993; Marshall and Rossman 1999).

I gave much thought to the handling of staff distress, should it occur. Edwards (1993) describes situations where she has encountered research participants who have been disturbed for a number of days following a research interview. In the information-giving phase of the study, the nature of the interview, the topics likely to undergo discussion and my role and responsibilities to participants would be clearly explained. I also proposed to liaise with occupational health and counselling services to alert them to the study and to discuss how staff could access these services should the need arise.

Researchers cannot be impartial observers when undertaking an in-depth interview. Researchers and participants alike cannot escape making judgements and decisions based on the interview context. Such interviews are therefore inherently interactive. They produce data *because* of the interaction, not despite it. Thus, any notion of interviewer as collector of 'pure' data is flawed (Cicourel 1974; Fontana and Frey 2000; Silverman 2001). I therefore believed it appropriate to intervene in the event of a participant becoming distressed. To not do so would also, in my view, constitute an avoidance of ethical responsibility in relation to the safety and wellbeing of research participants. I proposed that should any participant become distressed I would halt the interview and offer support. Once composed, the participant could choose whether or not to continue with the interview. All participants would be made aware of various avenues of support available to them.

Minimising threat of sanction

All practising health care staff have a duty of care and are accountable to their professional bodies and/or employers for actions and decisions made in the context of their professional roles. It is therefore arguable that practices and decision making in relation to patients' sexual health are not private matters for practitioners but clinical concerns, open to scrutiny and debate, the same as any other area of clinical practice and decision making. However, for reasons outlined earlier, this could not be taken for granted.

Confidentiality and anonymity of research participants are important considerations. These were being offered in order to minimise any unwarranted reprisals that staff may have otherwise suffered if others learned of their participation or details of their contributions. Be that as it may, I was in a position where I could not offer confidentiality and anonymity in all situations. As a registered nurse I continue to be bound by a professional code of conduct (UKCC 1998). This requires me to report any matter or incident that threatens the safety of patients, colleagues or the public. Additionally, the organisation was allowing me access to conduct the study via an honorary contract and this also required me to report any such matters. In order to clarify this issue in more detail and come to a shared understanding of its practical ramifications, it was agreed with those internal to the organisation that regular meetings would take place between me, my supervisor and a senior manager of the organisation. We would negotiate what material would be considered 'reportable', a process by which I could have access to advice about potential and actual scenarios and by which I would report matters should the need ever arise. The details of these arrangements would also be shared with all potential and actual participants.

ETHICAL APPROVAL: FORMAL APPLICATION ISSUES

This study required the direct participation of staff and not patients. Guidelines about consent to research participation have generally been drawn up with patients in mind, rather than staff. In this case, staff were the direct subjects of the research, with patients as the indirect beneficiaries. Literature about ethical issues in research emphasises the protection of the vulnerable. Although staff may not be considered a vulnerable group in the same way as patients, they too can be exposed to exploitation and harm as research subjects as outlined above. Hence, just as researchers have ethical responsibilities towards patients who take part in research they also have the same responsibilities towards staff participants.

All research proposals involving NHS patients or health care staff must be subject to examination by a Research Ethics Committee (REC). Local Research Ethics Committees (LRECs) and Multi-centre Research Ethics Committees (MRECs) offer an independent review of ethical issues raised by proposed research (DoH 2001). Their judgements are based upon the principles of informed consent, confidentiality, anonymity, beneficence and non-maleficence and the voluntary nature of research participation as formalised by the Declaration of Helsinki (World Medical Association1996). The measures proposed in this study were underpinned and justified by these principles and were thought to demonstrate a sensitive application of and orientation to the wellbeing of research participants. These are vital components to be addressed in demonstrating ethical research practice and are fundamental to securing REC approval.

At the time of writing the original proposal and seeking ethical approval, there was no requirement to seek the permission of individual patients in order to peruse case notes. However, case notes were to be analysed within ward areas to maintain the confidentiality and physical security of the documents. All data were to be made anonymous. In the case of documents these would be made anonymous at the point of data collection. Tape-recorded interviews, where necessary, would be made anonymous immediately after their completion. All collected data would be stored in secure conditions compliant with the Data Protection Acts, separately from any identifying keys and with access restricted to the researcher. In this way the research should not lead to the identification of patients or staff.

Submissions to the REC included the relevant application forms, a full proposal with methods as identified above and an expanded discussion of the ethical considerations as outlined in this chapter. Samples of informed consent sheets, introductory letters and additional information request sheets were also included. In addition an undertaking to work with staff for a substantial time to build trust was submitted alongside details specifying how the organisation would be consulted about potential and actual publications stemming from the research findings.

THE RESPONSE

After 22 months, 17 letters, 20 e-mails and at least 10 telephone conversations between various parties I was no nearer to gaining ethical approval than when I first began to prepare for the study in the autumn of 1998. Ethical approval for the research was denied on four occasions within one year. Over the period of 22 months I was presented with various reasons for rejection, most of which were either concerns about methodology, policy issues or resource issues. These are presented below.

First proposal: reasons for rejection

The proposal first went before the Research Ethics Committee (REC) in August 1999. At the Committee's request, accompanied by my academic supervisor, I attended a meeting to discuss issues raised. The outcomes were not positive and the proposal was rejected. The reasons for rejection were received in December and included the following (all identifying information has been removed from these verbatim quotes):

- We are unclear what inferences could be drawn in a one-centre study sample. Other [organisation] care for mentally disordered offenders and a multi-centre study would perhaps be more effective if the inferences are to be meaningful.

- Staff's personal attitudes to sexuality is an area within which it would be difficult to work, and which people would be reluctant to discuss openly and honestly, self report on personal attitudes to sexuality being notoriously unreliable.

- As part of the Ethics Committee remit we are concerned to protect staff as well as patients and as you have been unable to provide us with a list of hypotheses we are not prepared to give a blank cheque as it were to research of this nature.

- You mention in Section 3 of the proposal 'evidence to suggest that practitioners accept sexuality as a legitimate area to include in patient care but have difficulty with those aspects', but provide no further information. Indeed, you say throughout that there is a problem of this nature at [the organisation] but provide no evidence. We are not prepared to accept this at face value.

- Whilst the theoretical approach you adopt is not of direct concern to the Committee insofar as you should adopt your own preferred method for your research, it is of concern when we consider the Ethical implications, which we are required to do. As you seem unwilling to spell out in detail the aims, methods and hypotheses we require before granting approval, we are not prepared to allow this research to go ahead. The Committee were very clear on this; we have a duty to protect the [organisation], staff and patients from research which could be harmful. Unless we know the details of what we are approving we are not prepared to give the go ahead. (REC 1999a, 1999b)

It had already been explained to the REC on more than one occasion and in various forms that exploratory studies aim to describe practice from which research hypotheses might eventually be generated. Typically, research of the nature proposed did not aim to produce statistical findings that are generalisable outside of the research setting. However, the findings might be of considerable use to the organisation, although my own view was that the research would be relevant to other in-patient settings since exploratory studies such as the one proposed tend to generate implications that might be more widely addressed.

It could not be known that staff would be reluctant to participate; rather, that might be a finding of the study. Other researchers had successfully researched sensitive topics and I had taken considerable steps to maximise open and frank discussions by reducing threat. Similarly, whether there was a 'problem' or not was not the focus of the study. Nor was it my claim that a local problem existed in relation to any sexual health aspects of patient care. Rather, staff's perceptions about patient need and clinical practice were at the heart of the inquiry. An identification of a 'problem' might emerge from the data, but this in itself was a matter for empirical study and could not be 'known' in advance.

Two further ethical questions arose from this interaction with the REC. Should they be making judgements about the scientific validity of peer-reviewed studies? What is the scope of legitimate protection of subjects and when does this equate with inappropriate paternalism?

Second proposal

Following the REC's decision it was arranged for the proposed study to undergo the Department of Health's external peer-review process. The outcome was ongoing support for the proposed topic and research design. I therefore set about reapplying for ethical approval hoping that the positive peer review and the continued support for the study at national level would help to allay the REC's previous concerns.

The proposal was again rejected. This time there were no written objections or concerns with regard to the methodology or research design. The reasons given for rejection included the following (all identifying information has been removed from these verbatim quotes):

- The Ethics Committee is not in business to protect [the organisation] but the relationship of the professional to his or her patient must be critical. If consent is given, then research may lead to patients' records being analysable regarding professional performance and must require at least the consent and support of the professional groups involved. We would feel it extremely unlikely that any doctor or nurse would welcome such a project which may inadvertently assess his professional performance.

- There was concern expressed about the possible repercussions to staff and staff morale. Access to patient records may well inadvertently describe aspects of the staff's views on sexuality and, in particular, those staff, past and present, who have not given their permission for their notes about patients to be examined.

- Additionally, the Committee was concerned about the cost to [the organisation]of this project. It appears that you will want to review 80–85 patients' records and interview countless members of staff. This would involve you in being escorted whilst you are in the secure area of [the organisation]. The finance department would need to be informed about the additional funds being sought even were this approved. (REC 2000a)

It is of note that these objections were equally applicable to the original proposal submitted in August 1999, yet the LREC had made no mention of these objections at that time.

Replies to the REC were sent explaining that there was no requirement for an escort because of the status of my honorary contract. It was also explained how the documentary analysis proposed could not be used to assess performance. The REC was asked to clarify why and how past employees' consent was necessary in order to peruse patient notes. No acknowledgement or explanations regarding these points were received. Correspondence merely reaffirmed '…their previous refusal to grant consent' (REC 2000b).

It is not normally the case for researchers examining patients' notes to have to obtain the permission of all individual practitioners who have made written entries into them – not even when the topic of inquiry has been sexual health. The authors of written entries within patients' notes are not the owners of them. Legally all the entries belong to the record itself. Of course the REC's stance could be explained as merely being conscientious about compliance with the Data Protection Acts. However, if this was the case it could have denied ethical approval for the analysis of patient records and allowed me to continue with the other aspects of the study. After all, the analysis of patients' notes was a small part of the study and no objections had been raised with regard to the other data collection methods being proposed. Following a further telephone conversation I learned of additional reasons for the REC's rejection. Again, these had not been mentioned previously:

- The REC didn't understand the proposed qualitative methodology.

- The REC was concerned about how findings might reflect on the organisation.

Now there were two sets of reasons for rejection – both questionable and neither completely compatible with the other. This lack of congruent advice and information left me at a loss to know how to proceed in order to satisfy the REC's concerns and obtain its approval. The situation prompted my supervisor and I to write another, joint letter to the REC requesting that it give all the reasons for rejection with a suitable explanation. The reply received did not answer any of our questions:

> At the recent Ethics Committee meeting held on 24 August 2000 your proposal was again discussed but it was felt that our original decision to decline approval for your request was the correct one.
>
> However, the Committee would be willing to consider a new application which met the Committee's requirements. (REC 2000c).

MAKING SENSE OF THE EXPERIENCE

I think there are two interpretations to be made of the above:

1. The REC was anxious to be conscientious in its responsibility to research subjects, and its only concern was legitimate protection and a commitment to high quality research.

2. The REC's views were a response to a perceived threat of political sanction. Although couched in terms of ethical argument, scientific validity and policy interpretation, the aim of the response could equally be interpreted as intending to prevent the implementation of sensitive research which had the potential to produce findings which might cause embarrassment and sanction within the organisation.

Readers are left to decide for themselves which one is the most likely. I raise here several issues that may be relevant. A reply detailing answers to our queries about the last set of objections has never been received – yet surely a conscientious REC would strive to demonstrate openness and transparency? A freely functioning REC should be able to give clear and consistent objections as reasons for rejection of a proposal. The fact that this was not forthcoming also raises questions about how such committees understand their responsibilities in relation to research that has competed professionally and academically to be supported by public funds. Additionally how is it that the REC could overturn on methodological grounds a study that has been approved on those same grounds by at least four separate experts in the field? Ramcharan and Cutcliffe (2001) note how RECs can mistakenly judge the emerging design of qualitative research to be concomitant with poor design and in turn brand these studies unethical. The effect is one of disadvantaging some research methods and privileging others.

PERSONAL RAMIFICATIONS

It is difficult to be objective about all the personal ramifications of these experiences. In my own case I certainly began to doubt my own capabilities in the face of repeated rejections from a public body constituted to pronounce on ethics. Whilst my experiences were disappointing and disempowering they could not be considered unique given the fate of many a researcher pursuing sensitive areas of inquiry. Although there were many barriers that, in isolation, may have been surmountable, cumulatively they perhaps paved the way for substantial problems and created an almost impenetrable wall. In more unhappy moments it seemed that my attempts to receive clear and consistent advice in order to move the research forward only resulted in my being demonised in the eyes of some.

However, my experiences left me with the stark question of what to do. In the absence of an unambiguous REC appeals process and in consultation with my supervisor, other close colleagues and the funding agency, I decided to abandon the proposed study – a Hobson's choice really, but I did not give up. I designed a fresh study on the same topic but one that would not require scrutiny by RECs. This has been satisfactorily achieved but at the cost of limiting the scope of the study and elements of the original methodology. Whilst I cannot say that I successfully overcame the barriers to my original study, I am able to say that I did survive the protracted period of turmoil and achieved my original goal, albeit by a different route. The new study progressed well and relatively smoothly. The quality of the data collected surpassed all expectations and this has been particularly satisfying in itself.

RAMIFICATIONS FOR PRACTICE AND RESEARCH

Sensitive issues like patients' sexual health will not go away. If these issues are not attended to in clinical practice then arguably serious problems, such as those that arose at Ashworth Hospital (Fallon et al. 1999), could be repeated. More generally, the diversity of sexual lifestyles and choices are such that sexual health research in the future is likely to explore more of the controversial not less. Arguably, then, sexual health research will at least remain sensitive but possibly become even more so.

Exploration of personal experiences and lifestyle choices could in effect increase even further the number of qualitative research proposals that RECs receive. For this reason committees may require training and information about sensitive research and qualitative research methods. My point is that there is a danger that ignorance about qualitative research methodologies, combined with political concerns about sensitive topics, may result in vital research being marginalised or neglected to the detriment of society's more vulnerable citizens. Health care workers will in addition be left with limited evidence from which to gauge best practice.

Additionally, more researchers will be driven to do what I have done – that is, to access research samples in a manner that does not require ethical approval. The new Research Governance Framework (DoH 2001) will make this option somewhat harder to achieve within health and social care domains but it is also making attempts to help level the playing field for qualitative researchers. However, the recommendation for a minimum of one member with social science expertise out of the 12 to 18 that will make up a REC gives little guarantee that qualitative researchers can have confidence in the process. It also takes little account of the volume of qualitative proposals being sent to those committees.

SENSITIVE RESEARCH AND RESEARCH ETHICS COMMITTEES: THE PRESENT AND FUTURE

There has been some concern recently that, outside of the UK, those expected to pronounce on the ethics of studies can be vulnerable to hierarchical power differences and political agendas which in turn can undermine independent review (Ashcroft and Pfeffer 2001). Within the UK such a situation, whether imagined or real, is more likely to be perceived when NHS LRECs are largely comprised of clinical and managerial personnel from the same NHS Trusts. The restructuring and formation of RECs as set out in the Research Governance Framework (DoH 2001) will certainly help to limit this potential. However, it is too early to judge whether the proposed changes will make the impact required in order to successfully address all of the issues examined within this chapter.

Fundamentally the new governance framework gives us more of the same not less. The process of ethical decision making is far from objective despite attempts to make it so (Robinson and Garratt 1999). This places REC members in a position of having to draw upon a diversity of existing moral and ethical principles. This is not an easy task but more transparency of process and reasoning would go some way to increasing confidence in the process of ethical review. Unfortunately, my experience demonstrates that a Research Ethics Committee can operate in a less than transparent and accountable manner when it does not articulate the arguments or basis for its decisions. In addition, the minutes of REC meetings are to remain confidential and their discussions private (DoH 2001). A standardised, formal complaints or audit procedure applicable to all RECs does not exist but would be one way of redressing this balance. Of course, this in itself raises questions about the kind of appeals process that should exist.

Some changes for the better have begun but there remains much to be striven for. The Department of Health has launched consultations on 'An Ethical Review of Social Care Research'. I hope that some of the issues raised here will contribute to those discussions. Principally a culture is required where RECs are required to work in collaboration and reciprocally with researchers to ensure that research is implemented with the highest regard and respect for the rights and freedoms of all those involved. The task to be mastered is one of RECs providing a quality service to organisations, patients and practitioners and not just a set of burning hoops to be jumped through by researchers.

REFERENCES

Ashcroft, R. and Pfeffer, N. (2001) 'Ethics Behind Closed Doors: Do Research Ethics Committees Need Secrecy?' *British Medical Journal 322*, 1294–1296.

Bergen, R.K. (1993) 'Interviewing Survivors of Marital Rape: Doing Feminist Research on Sensitive Topics.' In C. Renzetti and R.M. Lee (eds) *Researching Sensitive Topics*. Newbury Park, USA: Sage Publications.

Blom-Cooper, L. *et al.* (1992) *Report of the Committee of Inquiry into Complaints about Ashworth Hospital*. London: HMSO.

Cicourel, A. (1974) *Theory and Method in a Study of Argentine Fertility*. New York: Free Press.

Davison, S. (1999) 'Sexuality.' In P. Taylor and T. Swan (eds) *Couples in Care and Custody*. Oxford: Butterworth Heinemann.

DoH (2001) *Research Governance Framework for Health and Social Care*. London: The Stationery Office.

Edwards, R. (1993) 'An Education in Interviewing: Placing the Researcher and the Research.' In C. Renzetti and R.M. Lee (eds) *Researching Sensitive Topics*. Newbury Park, USA: Sage Publications.

Fallon, P., Bluglass, R., Edwards, B. and Daniels, G. (1999) *Report of the Committee of Inquiry into the Personality Disorder Unit, Ashworth Special Hospital (Executive Summary)*. London: The Stationery Office.

Fontana, A. and Frey, J. (2000) 'The Interview: From Structured Questions to Negotiated Text.' In N.K. Denzin and Y.S. Lincoln (eds) *Handbook of Qualitative Research* (2nd edition). Thousand Oaks, USA: Sage Publications.

Gamel, C., Davis, B. and Hengeveld, M. (1993) 'Nurses' Provision of Teaching and Counselling on Sexuality: A Review of the Literature.' *Journal of Advanced Nursing 18*, 1219–1227.

Glaser, B. (1992) *Basics of Grounded Theory Analysis.* Mill Valley, CA: Sociology Press.

Glaser, B. and Strauss, A. (1967) *The Discovery Of Grounded Theory: Strategies for Qualitative Research.* New York, USA: Aldine De Gruyter.

Gostin, L. (2000) 'Human Rights of Persons with Mental Disabilities.' *International Journal of Law and Psychiatry 23*, 2, 125–159.

Kaye, C. and Franey, A. (1999) 'Changing the Spots Tackling the Culture.' In C. Kaye and A. Franey (eds) *Managing High Security Psychiatric Care.* London: Jessica Kingsley Publishers.

Lee, R.M. (1993) *Doing Research on Sensitive Topics.* London: Sage Publications Ltd.

Markham, G. (2000) 'Policy and Service Development Trends: Forensic Mental Health and Social Care Services.' *Tizard Learning Disability Review 5*, 2, 26–31.

Marshall, C. and Rossman, G. (1999) *Designing Qualitative Research* (3rd edition). Thousand Oaks, USA: Sage Publications.

Morse, J. and Field, P. (1996) *The Application of Qualitative Approaches to Nursing Research* (2nd edition). London: Chapman and Hall.

Rae, M. (1993) 'Freedom to Care.' Ashworth Special Hospital.

Ramcharan, P. and Cutcliffe, J. (2001) 'Judging the Ethics of Qualitative Research: Considering the "Ethics as Process" Model.' *Health and Social Care in the Community 9*, 6, 358–366.

REC (1999a) Personal Communication, 28 September 1999.

REC (1999b) Personal Communication, 8 December 1999.

REC (2000a) Personal Communication, 22 March 2000.

REC (2000b) Personal Communication, 12 May 2000.

REC (2000c) Personal Communication, 6 September 2000.

Renzetti, C. and Lee, R.M. (1993) 'The Problems of Researching Sensitive Topics: an Overview and Introduction.' In C. Renzetti and R.M. Lee (eds) *Researching Sensitive Topics.* Newbury Park, USA: Sage Publications.

Robinson, D. and Garratt, C. (1999) *Introducing Ethics.* Cambridge: Icon Books Ltd.

Rodgers, J. (1999) 'Trying to Get it Right: Undertaking Research Involving People with Learning Difficulties.' *Disability and Society 14*, 4, 421–433.

Sieber, J. (1993) 'The Ethics and Politics of Sensitive Research.' In C. Renzetti and R.M. Lee (eds) *Researching Sensitive Topics.* Newbury Park, USA: Sage Publications.

Sieber, J. and Stanley, B. (1988) 'Ethical and Professional Dimensions of Sensitive Research.' *American Psychologist 43*, 735–741.

Silverman, D. (2001) *Interpreting Qualitative Data* (2nd edition). London: Sage Publications.

Special Hospitals Service Authority (1992) *Advisory Committee on Patient Relationships Within Special Hospitals* (Interim Report). London: SHSA.

Stacey, J. (1988) 'Can There Be a Feminist Ethnography?' *Women's Studies International Forum 11*, 1, 21–27.

Swan, T. and Taylor, P. (1999) *Couples in Care and Custody.* London: Butterworth Heinemann.

Symonds, B. (1998) 'The Philosophical and Sociological Context of Mental Health Care Legislation.' *Journal of Advanced Nursing 27*, 946–954.

Taylor, P. (1998) 'Patients as Intimate Partners: Resolving a Policy Crisis.' In C. Kaye and A. Franey (eds) *Managing High Security Psychiatric Care.* London: Jessica Kingsley Publishers.

Tiefer, L. (1995) *Sex is Not a Natural Act.* Oxford: Westview Press.

UKCC (1998) *Code of Professional Conduct.* London: UKCC.

World Health Organisation (1986) *Concepts for Sexual Health* (EUR/ICP/MCH 521). Copenhagen: World Health Organisation.

World Health Organisation (1987) *Concepts of Sexual Health, Report of a Working Group Convened by the World Health Organisation (EURO).* Copenhagen: World Health Organisation.

World Medical Association (1996) *Declaration of Helsinki.* South Africa: World Medical Association.

The Contributors

Gwen Adshead is a forensic psychiatrist and psychotherapist working at Broadmoor Hospital. She has a Masters Degree in Medical Law and Ethics and has been involved in writing and teaching about ethics in mental health. She is currently Chair of the Ethics Committee of the Royal College of Psychiatrists.

Annie Bartlett, MA, Bchir, Mphil, MRCPsych, is a Senior Lecturer and Consultant in Forensic Psychiatry at St George's Hospital Medical School and Springfield University Hospital. She is additionally qualified in Social Anthropology. Her research interests include social theory applied to the practice of psychiatry, the study of institutions and evaluation of health services with particular reference to gender, ethnicity and sexual orientation. She is also Course Director of the MSc/Postgraduate Diploma in Forensic Mental Health at St George's Hospital Medical School.

Christine Brown is a psychiatrist with a reasearch background in social anthropology. She was awarded a Robert Baxter Research Fellowship from the National Programme for Forensic Mental Health Research and Developemnt in 1997 and has completed research examining the pathways into high security psychiatric care. She is currently a psychiatrist and reasearcher in the Mental Health Research Group, Institute of Health and Social Care at the Peninsula Medical School, Universities of Exeter and Plymouth.

Krysia Canvin is a postdoctoral qualitative researcher in the Department of Primary Care at the University of Liverpool. Her previous work includes the experience of pregnancy in prison, service users' experiences of compulsory community supervision, professional and lay perceptions of public involvement in clinical governance, and individuals' return to work following mental health related sickness absence. Her current interests lie in mental health and consumer involvement in policy-making, service delivery and research.

Caroline Logan is a Senior Baxter Research Fellow at the University of Liverpool. The National Programme on Forensic Mental Health Research and Development (NPFMHRD), which is a body within the Department of Health dedicated to the promotion of forensic mental health research, funds this fellowship. For this fellowship, Dr Logan is undertaking a five-year programme of research into risk assessment and management in male violent and sexually violent offenders in forensic and penal establishments. Dr Logan is a clinical psychologist by training and has a DPhil in experimental psychology.

Tom Mason, PhD, BSc (Hons), RMN, RNMH, RGN, has worked in forensic nursing in the UK for over 28 years predominantly, but not exclusively, in the high security psychiatric services. He has co-authored and co-edited eight books and published over seventy articles on numerous issues. He completed his PhD in 1995 and was awarded the International Association of Forensic Nurses Achievement Award in 1999. He is currently Professor of Forensic Nursing at the Caswell Clinic/University of Chester College of High Education.

Justine Rothwell is a Research Associate working for the University of Manchester. She has recently completed a longitudinal study looking at the mental health needs of boys in secure care. The first three years of the study have been published and submitted as her PhD. Her current post is on a randomised controlled trial evaluating the benefit of a group therapy programme for adolescents who repeatedly self-harm.

Jean Ruane is Lecturer and Research Fellow in Forensic Mental Health at the University of Sheffield. She has advised the Home Office, Department of Health and City Councils on various forensic mental health matters. Jean has also contributed to the development and validation of forensic programmes within her own and other universities. She is a nurse by background with a number of years clinical experience within high security care.

Carly Smith graduated in 1996 with a BSc in Psychology. She worked at the Adolescent Forensic Service as a research assistant until 2000 when she moved to the Adult Forensic Service to work as an assistant psychologist. She is currently employed by the Leeds Teaching Hospitals NHS trust in the capacity of Psychologist in Clinical Training. Her main research interests to date have been the interactions between psychosocial backgrounds and clinical presentations of clients presenting to services. She is particularly interested in the complex presentations of clients with schizophrenia and pervasive developmental disorders.

Subject Index

Author Index